Happy Cooking!
Becky

Cooking SOUP to NUTS

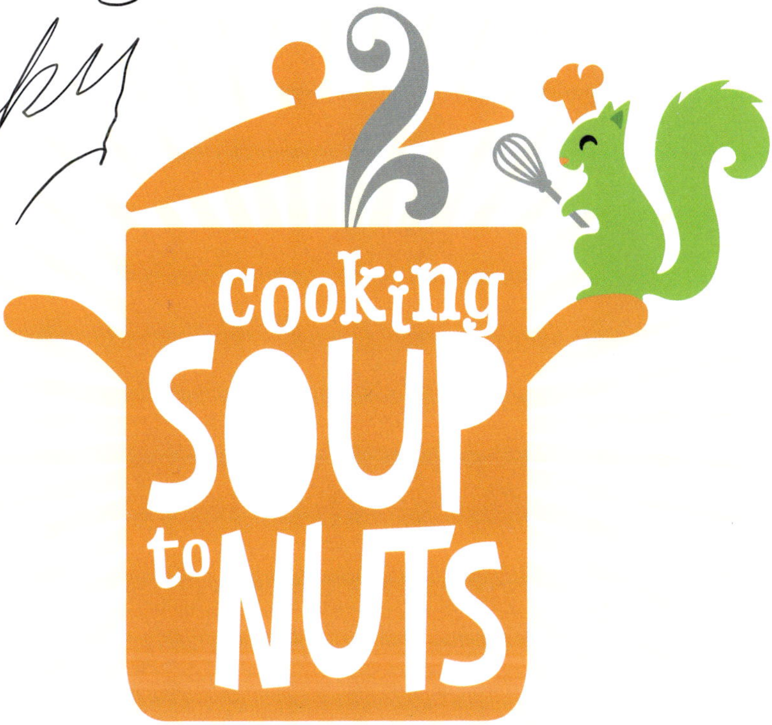

OVER 60 SOUP RECIPES TO MIX & MATCH WITH SALADS AND SANDWICHES FOR MOUTHWATERING COMBINATIONS

THAT ALL START WITH A POT OF SOUP

BY CHEF BECKY FOULK

www.CookingSoupToNuts.com

Dorrance Publishing Co
585 Alpha Drive
Suite 103
Pittsburgh, PA 15238
Visit our website at www.dorrancebookstore.com

ISBN: 978-1-4809-4005-5
eISBN: 978-1-4809-4028-4

Front & Back Cover Photographs by Dick Patrick - Dick Patrick Studios
www.dpatrick.com

Photographs on pages 14, 15, 17, 18, 23, 27, 29, 37, 38, 41, 49, 55, 56, 58, 73, 74, 85, 94, 97, 101,
102, 106, 113, 121, 122, 125, 142 and Back Cover by Becky Foulk.

Logo, Illustrations and Book Design by Nathan Ezra Trimm — theGHOSTCREATIVE
www.theghostcreative.com

This information was generated using the ReciPal nutritional program and
based on a 1 cup serving unless specified.
With the massive array of manufactured ingredients to choose from calories could vary.

ACKNOWLEDGMENTS

I would like to dedicate this book to my mom, Grace Foulk, who encouraged me from a very young age to experiment in the kitchen and follow that passion into a successful career. My mom loved soup and I think at one point she tasted every soup in this book. You were a great tester, kitchen helper and had the dishpan hands to go with it. I am truly blessed to have had you as my mom. Your guidance, love and support will be in my heart forever.

thank you

Dick Patrick

Thank you for taking the photo for the book's cover. You are an amazing talent and I am very lucky to call you a friend.

Ellen Elwell

Thank you for your friendship and mentoring. Your guidance and hours and hours of editing enabled me to bring my dream of writing a cookbook into reality.

Nathan Ezra Trimm

Your talent, creative energy and direction through the design process has helped me take my recipes and create a beautiful book. Thank you for everything and especially my little squire chef who I hope follows me through the rest of my career.

additional thanks

Donna Rains Clark - Copyeditor
Heather Williams - Agent for Dick Patrick Studios
Abe Thomas - Photo Retoucher from PiktuDigital

Lastly, I would like to thank all my friends and family for being great guinea pigs while I was finalizing the recipes for this book. I appreciate your support, feedback and HUNGRY STOMACHS!

a note from the chef

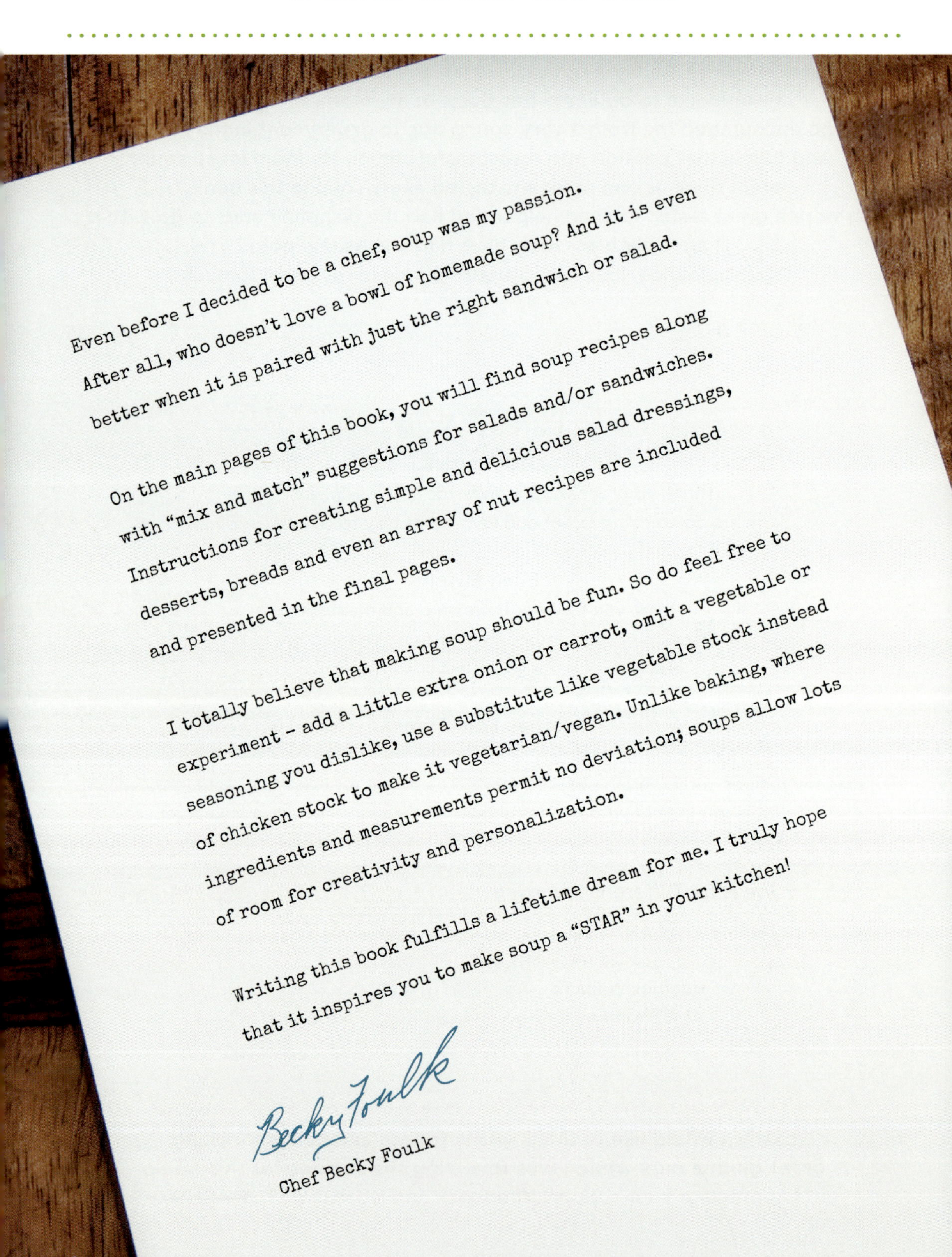
Even before I decided to be a chef, soup was my passion. After all, who doesn't love a bowl of homemade soup? And it is even better when it is paired with just the right sandwich or salad.

On the main pages of this book, you will find soup recipes along with "mix and match" suggestions for salads and/or sandwiches. Instructions for creating simple and delicious salad dressings, desserts, breads and even an array of nut recipes are included and presented in the final pages.

I totally believe that making soup should be fun. So do feel free to experiment - add a little extra onion or carrot, omit a vegetable or seasoning you dislike, use a substitute like vegetable stock instead of chicken stock to make it vegetarian/vegan. Unlike baking, where ingredients and measurements permit no deviation; soups allow lots of room for creativity and personalization.

Writing this book fulfills a lifetime dream for me. I truly hope that it inspires you to make soup a "STAR" in your kitchen!

Becky Foulk

Chef Becky Foulk

TABLE OF CONTENTS

the

BASICS

{ tips, tools & techniques }

IT ALL STARTS WITH A great SOUP POT

Making a well-balanced, fresh and tasty pot of soup is a "LABOR OF LOVE." It takes time and heart. So it's worth spending a bit extra on a quality pot that distributes heat quickly, provides an even cooking surface and lets you control the temperature.

RECOMMENDED SOUP POT FEATURES:

- A heavy-gauge bottom *(essential to prevent scorching)*
- 12-quart capacity *(if storage is a concern, an 8- or 6-quart is fine)*
- Stainless steel, enameled cast iron, or "hard-anodized" aluminum *(will not react to acidic foods, whereas an aluminum pot could react to highly acidic foods and metal utensils and create a grayish hue to a cream soup)*
- A nonstick, scratch-resistant surface *(great for easy cleaning)*
- A heat-resistant handle that is securely attached

OTHER ESSENTIAL EQUIPMENT:

- Handheld immersion *(stick)* blender — you can substitute a food mill, blender or food processor, but I find the stick easier than dealing with transferring hot soup from one container to the other
- A quality whisk
- High-heat *(silicone)* rubber spatulas
- Standard measuring spoons and cups
- A sharp, well-balanced 8- or 10-inch chef or santoku knife
- A quality cutting board to permit easy, safe cutting
- A fine mesh strainer, to eliminate cloudy stocks if making scratch stocks
- A handheld lemon/lime squeezer and a Microplane® zester

ABOUT THE HEAT:

- Start soups on medium-high heat for the initial sauté and blooming of the spices. This is the key to creating the foundation of flavors.
- Then reduce heat to medium or medium-low for a slow simmer, letting all flavors meld together.
  NOTE: Unless you are waiting on beans, grains or potatoes to cook, a good rule of thumb for simmering is a minimum of 15 to 20 minutes.

THICKENING THE SOUP:

Bringing the perfect texture/body to a soup is vital to achieving its maximum flavor. Too thick, soup will be heavy; too thin, soup will be watery and bland. Even a small amount of starch added to clear soups, like chicken noodle, helps maximize flavor.

There are many ways to thicken soups — classic roux, starch or flour slurry, pureeing, eggs, cream, beans, pastas, potatoes, bread and grains. Using the right thickening process is important for flavor and texture but also the ability to freeze, reheat, or hold heat for a period of time.

THE MAIN TECHNIQUES OF THICKENING USED IN THIS COOKBOOK ARE:

Roux

Equal parts of flour and butter/oil are cooked together. The longer the roux is cooked, the darker the color and nuttier the flavor. This is what I use mostly in production kitchens. However, when cooking at home and throughout this book, instead of making a roux on the side, I just sprinkle flour and blend with the initial vegetable and fat sauté. This "simple roux" needs to be cooked for several minutes and then slowly add and blend liquid into the mixture to eliminate any flour lumps.
NOTE: Substitute other flours like rice flour for gluten intolerance.

Starch

Blend starches with a cold liquid before adding to the soup, simmer 3-5 minutes. Use starches in only small quantities to add body. Be careful not to add too much, which creates a thick, slippery texture. When freezing cream soups, I find a small amount of starch helps prevent the cream from separating when reheated.
NOTE: Arrowroot, potato or tapioca starch can be substituted for the cornstarch in this book.

Puree

My favorite way to intensify flavor, add texture and avoid using flour is to puree. You can puree all or a portion of the soup depending on the desired texture and consistency.

THE INGREDIENTS

Soup ingredients don't have to be expensive. You can find quality fresh vegetables at the corner grocery store, local farmer's market, and club/discount stores. Produce for soup does not have to be the cream of the crop. A little blemish will go unnoticed and is usually less expensive. When prepared stocks, canned beans or tomatoes go on sale, it is a great time to stock your pantry.

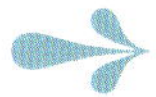

SOME NOTES ON THE KIND OF INGREDIENTS I PREFER AND HOW I PREP THEM FOR COOKING:

Canola Oil

I cook with canola oil. 100% of the oil comes from the canola plant and is considered to be one of the healthiest vegetable oils on the market. Having the lowest level of saturated fat, it is high in monounsaturated fats and contains omega 5 fatty acids.
NOTE: You can easily substitute any vegetable oil if you desire (all oils are 120 calories per tablespoon). Olive oil costs more and adds a distinct flavor that may or may not work with a specific soup. I would recommend that you use olive oil only when it is specifically called for in a recipe to add flavor and richness.

Kosher Salt

Compared to table salt, I find the larger, coarser grains of kosher salt to be less salty, have no metallic flavor, easier to sprinkle on food and best at bringing out natural flavors. As a rule of thumb, 1 Tbsp of kosher salt = 1 tsp salt.

Fresh Citrus

To enhance and round out the flavors in the soup, I like to add fresh citrus *(zest and juice)* at the end, along with the finishing herbs. Individual recipes will specify how much citrus zest and juice to use. With the tools on the market like the Microplane® and juicers, adding the citrus finish is quicker and easier.

Fresh Herbs

I prefer to use fresh herbs *(versus dried)* because there is a difference in the intensity of flavor.

A COUPLE OF NOTES:

- **"Sprigs"** — Many recipes call for a "sprig" of thyme or rosemary. It is my personal preference to put the entire sprig *(stem and leaves)* into the soup for cooking and remove it, along with the bay leaf, once the soup is finished. As a rule of thumb, a sprig of thyme = 1/6 of a standard grocery store bunch, 1 1/2 teaspoons fresh chopped, or 1/2 tsp dry leaf.
- **Finishing herbs** — Fresh parsley, cilantro, basil, and dill should be washed, chopped, and added toward the end of the cooking process. The finishing herbs still need to simmer in the soup for a couple of minutes to release their flavor and as a safety standard. These herbs lose intensity of flavor when simmered for a long time.

Canned Tomatoes and Beans

I use mostly fresh ingredients. Whenever a recipe calls for a canned item, however, use the smaller 14- to 15-ounce cans, unless specifically stated in the recipe. Purchase the lower sodium varieties, and I prefer to purchase organic varieties when available.

Canned Tomatoes:

There are many brands of tomatoes available, offering an array of different textures, colors and flavors. Many chefs rave about San Marzano tomatoes from Italy. However, I find that many American brands taste great and can be more economical, especially if you stock up on sales. *NOTE: When buying diced tomatoes, look for the petite size cut, it will blend better with other diced vegetables in the pot.*

Canned Beans:

The specific variety of bean required for a soup is indicated in the recipe, but regardless of the type, always drain and rinse them. You may prefer to substitute dried beans for any canned bean in a recipe. The beans need to be cooked before adding. If you have a pressure cooker, raw beans can be cooked in as little as 8 to 12 minutes. As a rule of thumb, one small can of drained beans = 1 1/2 cups of cooked.

Onions

I use whichever variety of seasonal sweet onion is available at the grocery store. There are a couple of recipes that specifically call for red onions, but you can substitute any variety for convenience.

Garlic

Fresh and chopped:

I prefer to peel and chop my own garlic. The flavor of freshly chopped adds to the depth of flavor in a recipe. *NOTE: Don't chop and store garlic in oil in the refrigerator for any length of time — it can grow harmful bacteria. A good rule of thumb, a normal size garlic clove = 1 teaspoon chopped garlic.*

Grocery store chopped:

In-store chopped garlic is usually packed in water and preservatives. The water can cause the garlic to lose some of its intensity, and while it is convenient, it generally costs more.

CUTTING INSTRUCTIONS

Your goal is to cut all the vegetables close to the same size so they cook evenly and fit together in a soup spoon. To this end, each recipe has a combination of cutting instructions for different types of produce or specific cut sizes.

DICING

- When a recipe says "dice," it means 1/2-inch squares. However, you will find a smaller 1/4-inch dice for garnish so it scatters throughout the soup. And on occasion, 3/4-inch dices for a chunky texture.

STRAIGHT-CUT CELERY

- This type of cutting creates the natural half-moon shape, which adds a "homemade" touch. Use smaller stalks *(preferable)*. If using large outside stalks, split in half lengthwise before cutting.

CIRCLE-CUT CARROTS

- I prefer baby carrots because the smaller diameter pairs better with the 1/2-inch diced vegetables and fits in the spoon.
- **Julienne** — These strips should be 1/4- to 1/2-inch wide and no longer than 1 1/2 inches.

GREEN ONIONS

- Cut thin, 1/4-inch circles so they scatter evenly throughout the soup or salad and will not overwhelm the dish.

BROCCOLI & CAULIFLOWER FLORETS

- Usually used for garnish, these should be 1/2 to 3/4 inch for a perfect fit in the spoon.

FREEZING SOUP FOR ANOTHER DAY

It's always great to have a soup or two in the freezer for a quick and easy meal. The bonus of a large pot of soup is that there's plenty to freeze. The recipes in this book can easily be doubled or tripled to stock the freezer. The "life" for keeping frozen soups at optimal quality is 3 months.

NOTE: It's safe to eat the soup after a much longer period, but the overall texture and flavor does begin to diminish.

SOUPS MUST BE COOLED BEFORE FREEZING.

The easiest method is to place soup in an ice water bath in your sink. Make sure the cold water is at least level with the hot soup, stir often to speed up cooling. Cool to 45°F before packing.

ITEMS YOU WILL NEED:

- **Zip-closure freezer storage bags** take up less space in the freezer and are easy to stack flat once frozen. To fill: Open bag in a bowl or container and cuff the top over the sides to form a "mouth." Then fill, squeeze out air and seal. Lay flat on a tray and freeze. *NOTE: When ready to eat, remove bag from freezer, thaw overnight in refrigerator, then remove from the bag to reheat on the stovetop or in a microwave-safe container to a minimum of 165°F.*
- **FoodSaver® sealing bags** work great and the bags can usually be dropped directly in boiling water for easy reheating.
- **Individually portioned containers** are best for the lunch box and microwaving. Fill, top and freeze. Be sure to leave about a 3/4-inch air space to allow the soup to expand.
- **A permanent marker** is a must or you will be playing the guessing game. Before filling the containers, mark the soup name and date.

recipe index

SALADS

DRESSINGS, SPREADS & EXTRAS

NUTS {VG}

SWEETS

ICE CREAM TOPPINGS

= soup ingredients can be adjusted to be **Vegetarian** or **Vegan**

VG = **Vegan** – all plant-based ingredients with nothing derived from an animal

V = **Vegetarian** – vegan with dairy & eggs added

G = **Gluten Free** – items do not contain gluten — **double check any pre-prepared items that they are completely gluten free**

C = **Calorie Wise** – soups that are 225 calories or less for a 1 cup serving

Nutritional Guide – Refer to page 146

Apple Kale Salad

Jicama Orange Salad

Senate Bean Soup

Maple Baked Apples

Loaded Sweet Potato Soup

Pulled Pork + Kale Biscuit Sandwiches

the RECIPES

Classic Tomato Soup

Josh's Favorite
ROASTED EGGPLANT & TOMATO BISQUE

YIELDS: 2 1/4 QUARTS

2 quarts	Eggplant, peeled and large diced
2 quarts	Tomatoes, large diced
1 cup	Onions, diced
3-4 cloves	Garlic, smashed
1 cup	Basil - fresh, chopped *(use stems for roasting to add additional flavor)*
2 Tbsp	Canola Oil
1 1/2 quarts	Vegetable Stock *(page 131)*
1 can (6 oz)	Tomato Paste
1 cup	Heavy Cream
1 1/2 tsp	Kosher Salt
1 tsp	Black Pepper

- Heat oven to 385°F
- In a large bowl, toss the eggplant, tomatoes, onions, garlic, basil stems and half the salt and pepper in the canola oil
- Oil/spray sheet pan for easy cleanup
- Spread vegetables flat *(no piles)* on one or two trays for even cooking
- Roast vegetables for 20 minutes, stir and continue roasting until the vegetables smash with a spoon and are browning
- Remove from oven, cool slightly for easy handling
- Remove the basil stems, and scrape mixture into a soup pot
- Add vegetable stock and tomato paste; bring to a boil over medium-high heat
- Reduce heat, simmer 10-15 minutes
- Puree with an immersion blender
- Add basil and cream
- Simmer for another 5 minutes
- Adjust seasoning to taste with salt and pepper

NOTE: If freezing, add 1 Tbsp Cornstarch blended with 1/4 cup water with basil and cream. This helps stop cream from separating when reheating.

TO MAKE PASTA SAUCE,
you want the consistency a little thicker:

- Reduce the vegetable stock amount to just 1 quart instead of 1 1/4 quarts
- Toss with pasta and shaved Parmesan or goat cheese
- Perfect with chicken, shrimp, Italian sausage or meatballs

Italian Vegetable Chopped Salad

SERVES: 2 TO 3 PEOPLE

SMALL DICE:

1 1/2 cups	Iceberg Lettuce
1 1/2 cups	Romaine Lettuce
1 cup	Tomatoes
1/2 cup	Cucumbers
1/4 cup	Artichoke Hearts

ADD:

1/2 cup	Chickpeas
1/4 cup	Quality Pitted Olives, chopped
1/4 cup	Asiago Cheese, small diced

TOSS WITH:

1/2 cup	Dressing — Italian, Red Wine or Pesto Vinaigrette *(page 134)*

ADD (OPTIONAL):

1 cup	Chicken Breast, Italian Salami, Ham or Shrimp

Parmesan Cheese Bread

1 loaf	Ciabatta* - split in half and place on a baking pan
1/4 cup	Olive Oil - brush each half with olive oil
1/2 tsp	Italian Seasoning** - lightly shake on top of bread
1/2 cup	Shredded Parmesan Cheese - sprinkle on top of bread

- Preheat oven to 375°F
- Bake 10–15 minutes, until cheese melts and bread is golden brown

*Substitute Rosemary, Multigrain, Garlic or Italian bread for Ciabatta.
**Substitute your favorite pesto for the Italian seasonings.

RED BEANS & RICE SOUP

YIELDS: 3 QUARTS

1 cup	Bacon, diced
1/2 cup	Onions, diced
2 tsp	Garlic
2 Tbsp	Flour
1 cup	Red Beans - dry *(best if soaked overnight)*
1/4 cup	Jalapeños, sliced in thin circles
1 sprig	Thyme - fresh
1	Bay Leaf
1/2 tsp	Black Pepper
1/2 tsp	Salt
1 can (10 oz)	Diced Tomatoes with Green Chilies, mild *(or hot for extra spice)*
2 quarts	Chicken Stock *(page 130)*
2 quarts	Water
2 Tbsp	Cornstarch, blended with 1/4 cup water
1/2 cup	Red Pepper, diced
1 1/2 cups	Rice*, cooked

- Heat a soup pot over medium heat; cook the bacon, remove to add back in later
- Add onions, sauté until they begin to sweat, then add garlic, cook until onions are translucent
- Sprinkle and blend in flour with onion mix, cook for 3 minutes
- Add jalapeños, red beans, herbs and spices, cook for 2 minutes
- Add the canned tomatoes, then slowly add chicken stock, blending all ingredients together
- Add water, bring to a boil, reduce heat and simmer until the red beans are tender *(1 to 1 1/2 hours)*
- Once tender, add the cornstarch, bacon and red peppers, simmer 4 minutes
- Adjust seasoning to taste with salt and pepper
- Fold in rice and serve

*I prefer Basmati rice for flavor and texture:
Add 3/4 cup rice to 1 1/2 cups water with a pinch of salt; bring to a boil, reduce heat and simmer until all water is absorbed (about 15 minutes); spread out on tray and cool completely. The rice should be al dente to stop It from becoming mushy In the hot broth.

Pulled Pork + Kale Biscuit Sandwiches

Citrus Pecan Salad

SERVES: 3 TO 5 PEOPLE

1 cup	Citrus*, peeled, sliced, seeds removed
3 cups	Baby Spinach
1/4 cup	Champagne or Honey Mustard Dressing *(page 134)*
1/4 cup	Candied Pecans *(page 141)*

- Toss the spinach with the dressing and place on a platter or individual plates
- Top with the citrus, then sprinkle with candied pecans
- **Optional:** Add blue or goat cheese or top salad with pulled pork

*Try a trio of citrus for a fun contrast in color and flavor.

Pulled Pork & Kale Biscuit Sandwiches

YIELDS: 12 MINI-SANDWICHES

12	Biscuits or Rolls
1 1/2 lb	Pulled Pork *(2 oz per sandwich)*
2 cups	Greens *(1 oz per sandwich)*

PORK*:

- Remove any large pieces of fat and rub a pork shoulder liberally with Cajun spices, then place in a roasting pan
- Cook pork at 400°F oven for 30 minutes until it begins to brown
- Reduce heat to 275°F, add 1 to 2 cups water to pan, cover with foil
- Roast until tender and pork begins to pull apart *(this could take 5–7 hours depending on the size of the pork)*
- Remove from oven, let it rest for a good 30 minutes, then pull with a fork

*If you prefer, make it easy and purchase pulled pork from your grocery store or favorite BBQ restaurant.

GREENS:

2 Tbsp	Canola Oil
1/2 cup	Onions, thin julienne
1 tsp	Garlic, chopped
2 quarts	Kale or other greens, washed and cut into 1/2-inch strips
1/8 tsp	Crushed Red Pepper Flakes
1/2 tsp	Kosher Salt

- Heat a braising pan over medium-high heat with canola oil
- Add onions and begin to sauté
- Add garlic, salt and crushed red pepper, then add greens
- Sauté greens until they are wilted and tender
- Adjust seasoning to taste with salt and pepper
- **Optional:** Add 1 tsp grainy mustard

ASSEMBLY:

- Split a warm, freshly baked biscuit or roll
- Fill with pulled pork and top with wilted greens
- **Optional:** Add cheddar cheese and serve with your favorite spicy mustard

Butternut Squash & Apple Bisque

YIELDS: 2 QUARTS

1/4 cup	Canola Oil
1/2 cup	Leeks, diced
1 cup	Apples, peeled and large diced
1 1/2 Tbsp	Sage, fresh chopped
1 sprig	Thyme - fresh
1	Bay Leaf
2 cups	Butternut Squash, peeled and cubed
1/2 tsp	Kosher Salt
1/4 tsp	Black Pepper
1 quart	Vegetable Stock *(page 131)*
1 cup	Apple Cider
1 cup	Heavy Cream*
1 Tbsp	Cornstarch, blended with 1/4 cup water

GARNISH:

1 cup	Apples, peeled and small diced
1 Tbsp	Parsley, chopped

- Heat a soup pot over medium-high heat
- Add the canola oil, leeks, apples, squash, sage, thyme, bay leaf, salt and pepper
- Sauté until the vegetables begin to sweat
- Add the vegetable stock and apple cider
- Bring to a boil, reduce heat, simmer until the squash is soft
- Puree soup with immersion blender until smooth
- Garnish with apples and parsley and add cream
- Adjust seasoning with salt and pepper to taste
- Add cornstarch, cook for 5 minutes
- **Optional:** Sprinkle the top with toasted pepitas *(pumpkin seeds)* and/or dried cranberries for added color and crunch

*Make It vegan - substitute coconut or almond milk for cream.

A GREAT SOUP TO SERVE FOR THANKSGIVING!

Perfect Fall Salad

SERVES: 1 PER PERSON

TOSS TOGETHER:

1 cup	Field Greens
1/4 cup	Pear, sliced
1 1/2 Tbsp	Blue Cheese
1 Tbsp	Candied Pecans *(page 141)*
2 Tbsp	Balsamic Vinaigrette *(page 135)*

FOR INDIVIDUAL PLATES:

- Toss the field greens with the dressing and plate
- Top each plate with pear slices in the center with blue cheese and Candied Pecans sprinkled around the pear

Turkey Cranberry Wrap

SERVES: 1 TO 2 PEOPLE

1	Tortilla, 8- or 10-inch
2 Tbsp	Cranberry Cream Cheese
1 Tbsp	Walnuts, toasted and roughly chopped *(optional)*
1/2 cup	Spinach Leaves
3 slices	Turkey Breast (2 oz)
1/4	Apple, thinly sliced

- Warm tortilla in a pan or microwave until pliable
- Spread cranberry cream cheese, covering entire tortilla
- **Optional:** Sprinkle with toasted walnuts
- Arrange the spinach over 3/4 of the wrap
- Top with the turkey, then thinly sliced apples
- Roll the tortilla toward the 1/4 that is spread with cream cheese

Cranberry Cream Cheese

1 cup	Whipped Cream Cheese
2 Tbsp	Dried Cranberries, chopped
2	Clementines, zest and juice

- Place cranberries and clementine zest and juice in a microwave container
- Heat for 30 to 45 seconds
- Cool and fold into cream cheese

AZTEC CHICKEN SOUP

YIELDS: 3 1/2 QUARTS

1/4 cup	Canola Oil
2 cups	Chicken Breast, diced
1 cup	Onions, diced
1 cup	Carrots, diced
1/2 cup	Celery, diced
1 tsp	Cumin
1/2 tsp	Chili Powder
1/2 tsp	Paprika
1/2 tsp	Salt
1/2 tsp	Black Pepper
1/4 tsp	Chipotle Powder
2 cups	Chunky Salsa Verde
1 can (14.5 oz)	Fire Roasted Tomatoes
2 quarts	Chicken Stock *(page 130)*
2/3 cup	Raw Quinoa, rinsed
4 Tbsp	Cilantro

- Heat a soup pot over medium-high heat with canola oil
- Add chicken, season with salt and pepper, and lightly brown
- Add onions and spices, cook for 2 minutes
- Add carrots and celery, sauté until vegetables begin to sweat
- Add salsa, tomatoes and chicken stock
- Bring to a boil, reduce heat and simmer 10 minutes
- Add rinsed quinoa, simmer 12–15 minutes
- Add cilantro and season to taste with salt and pepper
- Serve soup with a wedge of lime

Quinoa

This soup is thickened with Quinoa.
CONSIDERED A SUPER GRAIN FOR ITS PROTEIN CONTENT,
quinoa contains a perfect balance of all nine amino acids essential for human nutrition, which is rarely found in plant-based foods. Quinoa also offers a good dose of fiber and iron.

Quinoa seeds are coated with saponin, a bitter substance that protects the seeds from predators. Most likely the quinoa you purchase is rinsed, but as a best practice give it a rinse.

Avocado Toast

SERVES: 1 PER PERSON

1 slice	Whole Grain Bread
1/2	Avocado
1 Tbsp	Salsa Verde
To taste	Kosher Salt
To taste	Black Pepper
3 to 4	Cilantro Leaves
1 Tbsp	Tomato, diced

- Toast the bread
- In a bowl, smash avocado with a fork
- Blend with the salsa, salt and pepper
- Spread the avocado mix on top of toast
- Top with tomato and cilantro leaves
- Optional: Add cheese or bacon

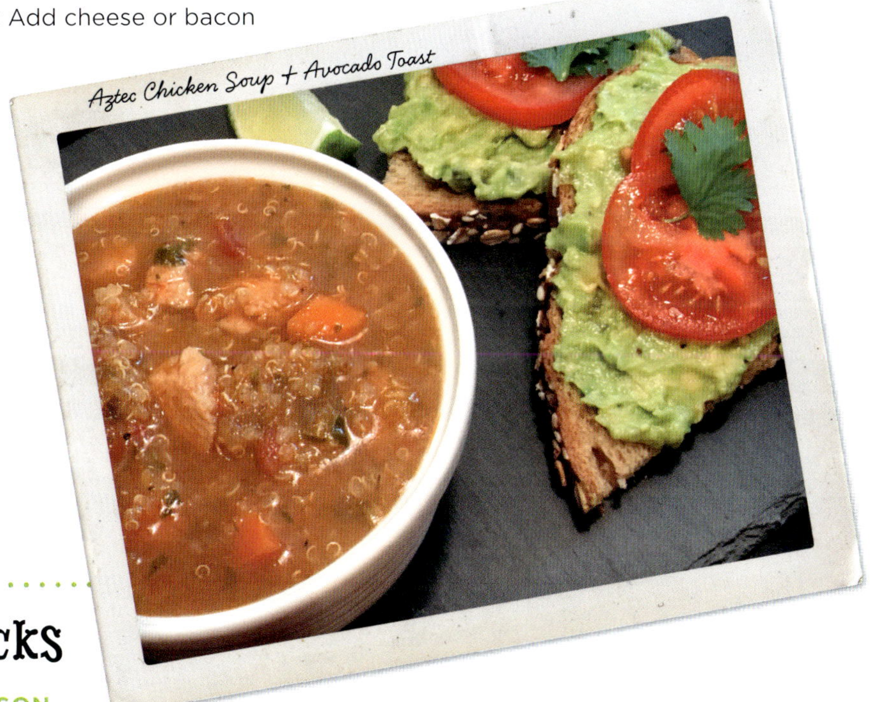

Jicama Sticks

SERVES: 1 PER PERSON

- Peel and cut jicama into finger-size sticks, place in a storage container
- Squeeze fresh orange and lime juice over the top
- Lightly sprinkle with salt, smoked paprika and chopped cilantro
- Stir and let sit for at least 20 to 30 minutes

 **KEEP IN THE REFRIGERATOR AS A GO-TO SNACK!**

CABBAGE PATCH SOUP

YIELDS: 3 QUARTS

1/4 cup	Canola Oil
12 oz	Smoked Sausage or Kielbasa, half-moon
1 cup	Onions, julienne
1/2 cup	Celery, sliced 1/4 inch
1/2 cup	Carrots, circle cut
1 tsp	Garlic, minced
5 cups	Cabbage, strips
1/2 cup	Green Pepper, diced
1 can (14.5 oz)	Fire Roasted Tomatoes
1 1/2 cups	Red Skin Potatoes, half-moon
1 strip	Thyme - fresh
1 sprig	Rosemary - fresh
2	Bay Leaves
1/2 tsp	Kosher Salt
1/2 tsp	Black Pepper
2 1/2 quarts	Chicken Stock *(page 130)*
2 Tbsp	Tomato Paste
1 Tbsp	Cornstarch, blended with 1/4 cup water
2 Tbsp	Red Wine Vinegar

- Heat a soup pot over medium-high heat and add canola oil
- Lightly brown the sausage, then add the onions, garlic, celery and carrots
- Light sauté and add the cabbage, green peppers, herbs, salt and pepper
- Once the cabbage begins to sweat, add the tomatoes, potatoes, chicken stock and tomato paste
- Bring to a boil and let simmer until the potatoes just begin to get soft
- Add the cornstarch and vinegar and let simmer a good 5 minutes
- Add salt and pepper to taste

i love making this soup on a crisp fall day!

- Serve with a loaf of rye or pretzel bread and sharp cheddar or Swiss cheese.
- Finish the meal with warm apple cranberry crisp and your favorite ice cream or cinnamon whipped cream.

Apple Cranberry Crisp

YIELDS: 3-QUART BAKING DISH

FILLING:

5 cups	Granny Smith Apples, peeled and diced
1 cup	Cranberries
2/3 cup	Sugar
1 Tbsp	Cinnamon - ground
1/4 tsp	Nutmeg
1	Lemon, zest and juice
2 Tbsp	Cornstarch, blended with 1/4 cup water

TOPPING:

1 1/2 cups	Flour
1 cup	Sugar
1/2 cup	Walnuts, toasted and chopped
1 cup	Rolled Oats
1 pinch	Salt
8 Tbsp	Butter, melted

FILLING:

- Preheat oven to 350°F
- Peel and dice apples and place in bowl with cranberries, sugar, cinnamon, nutmeg, cornstarch and lemon
- Toss and place in a sprayed baking pan

TOPPING:

- In a bowl, stir all the dry ingredients together
- Add melted butter, toss with hands until dry mixture binds together in pea-size pieces
- Scatter crumble over the top of apples
- Bake for 45 to 50 minutes
- The apples should be soft and bubbling through the golden brown crumble
- Best served warm

Cinnamon Whipped Cream

1 cup	Heavy Cream
2 Tbsp	Sugar
1 tsp	Cinnamon - ground

- Place all ingredients in a chilled bowl
- Whisk until peaks form

SENATE BEAN SOUP

YIELDS: 2 QUARTS

Senate Bean Soup is served every day in the Senate cafeteria.
This custom goes back to the early 1900s. It is debated which senator asked for it.
In my time in D.C., this would always be a weekly feature.

For this heavy soup, pair with a lightly dressed salad of mixed greens or arugula and warm cornbread with honey butter.

THE KEY TO THE FLAVOR OF THIS SOUP IS SMOKY THICK-CUT BACON*.

- You can substitute ham bone or ham hock for the bacon, but watch the salt level
- For non pork eaters, substitute smoked turkey leg

*An easy trick to cutting bacon: place in freezer for about 30 minutes before cutting.

4 oz	Bacon, julienne
1/2 cup	Onion, diced
2 tsp	Garlic, chopped
2	Bay Leaves
2 Tbsp	Tomato Paste
1 lb	Dry White Beans* *(best soaked overnight)*
2 1/2 quarts	Chicken Stock *(page 130)*, may need 1/2 quart more
1 tsp	Kosher Salt
1 tsp	Black Pepper
1 sprig	Thyme - fresh

- Heat a soup pot over medium-high heat
- Sauté the bacon until it is thoroughly cooked
- Remove, place on paper towel to add back later for garnish
- Add the onions and garlic in the bacon drippings and sauté until they begin to sweat
- Add the white beans, thyme, bay leaf and tomato paste, sauté for about 2 minutes
- Add the chicken stock and bring to a boil
- Reduce heat and simmer until the white beans are tender *(approximately 1 hour)*
- Remove 1/4 of the beans for garnish and discard the thyme sprig and bay leaves
- Puree the rest of the soup mixture in the pot
- Add the bacon and beans back to the pot
- If thick, add stock or water to desired consistency
- Add salt and pepper to taste
- Let simmer an additional 5 minutes

*Soaking beans overnight will reduce cooking time and ease digestion.

Cornbread

YIELDS: 1 PAN

1 cup	Cornmeal
3/4 cup	All Purpose Flour
1 Tbsp	Sugar, granulated
1 1/2 tsp	Baking Powder
1/2 tsp	Baking Soda
1/4 tsp	Kosher Salt
6 Tbsp	Butter, melted
2	Eggs, large
1 1/2 cups	Buttermilk
1/2 cup	Corn, roughly chopped
2 Tbsp	Red Pepper, minced

- Preheat oven to 425°F
- Butter an 8-inch baking dish
- In a bowl, mix dry ingredients together
- In a separate bowl, whisk the eggs, buttermilk and melted butter
- Add wet ingredients to dry ingredients and fold together
  - mixture will be lumpy but should have no dry spots
- Add corn and red pepper and pour into buttered baking pan
- Bake for 20–25 minutes, until a toothpick comes out clean
- Let cool about 10 minutes and serve

OPTIONS:

- Substitute jalapeños for red pepper
- Add shredded cheddar or jack cheese
- Bake in mini-muffin or bundt pans

Honey Butter

- Fold 1 stick of softened butter with 1 Tbsp honey and a pinch of salt to taste

Senate Bean Soup

CORN CHOWDER

Corn Chowder is a staple all around the country, but every region seems to add their own unique touch. For me, growing up outside of Philadelphia, we would travel to the Amish Country around Lancaster County. They would serve fresh corn chowder with bacon or ham and usually chicken. After moving to Texas, I've become a big fan of the spicy kick from adding poblano peppers. Depending on the coast shrimp, crab, lobster, salmon and even smoked trout, take these simple flavors to a whole new level. Use this basic recipe and have fun creating your personal spin on a very tasty soup.

You can make this soup with frozen corn, but when corn is in season it is best to take the extra time to cut it off the cob and make a Corn Stock *(page 55)* **– THE FLAVOR IS WORTH THE TIME!**

PAIR WITH A SIMPLE SALAD AND SERVE WITH PIPING-HOT BISCUITS OR BREAD.

Basic Corn Chowder

YIELDS: 2 1/2 QUARTS

1/2 cup	Bacon, julienne
4 Tbsp	Butter
2 Tbsp	Canola Oil
1 cup	Onions, diced
1/2 cup	Green Peppers*
1/2 cup	Celery, diced
1/2 cup	Red Pepper, diced
1 tsp	Kosher Salt
1/2 tsp	Black Pepper
7 Tbsp	Flour
2 cups	Red Potatoes, diced
2 cups	Corn
1 sprig	Thyme - fresh
1	Bay Leaf
2 1/2 quarts	Chicken *(page 130)* or Corn Stock *(page 55)*
1 cup	Cream
2 Tbsp	Cornstarch, blended with 1/4 cup water

- Heat a soup pot over medium-high heat
- If using bacon, cook first and set aside to add back later
- Add the butter, canola oil, and onions, sauté until onions begin to sweat
- Add celery, green peppers, salt and pepper or spices, sauté until vegetables begin to sweat
- Sprinkle and blend flour into vegetable mixture, cook for 4 minutes
- Slowly add half the stock, blending with the vegetable mixture to eliminate any lumps
- Add bay leaf, thyme, corn, red peppers, potatoes and the rest of the stock
- Bring to boil, reduce heat, and simmer until the potatoes are tender
- Add cornstarch and cream, simmer for 4 minutes
- Adjust seasoning to taste with salt and pepper

*Substitute poblano pepper for added spice.

Corn Chowder

REGIONAL CHOWDERS

Southwest Poblano Corn Chowder

- Add additional 1/2 cup Roasted Poblano Peppers *(page 54)*, diced
- Add additional 1 tsp each Cumin, Chipotle and Ancho Powder with vegetable sauté
- Finish with 3 Tbsp Cilantro

Chicken & Corn Chowder

- Bacon - cook first, reserve to add with cream
- Use Chicken Stock *(page 130)*
- Add 1 cup pulled or diced Cooked Chicken when adding cream
- Finish with 2 Tbsp Parsley

Smoked Salmon & Corn Chowder

- Add 1 cup Hard Smoked Salmon
- Add 1/4 up front when sautéing onion and the rest when adding cream
- Finish with 2 Tbsp Fresh Dill

Lobster, Shrimp or Crab Chowder

- Sauté 1 Tbsp of Old Bay® Seasoning in place of salt and pepper
- Add 1 cup Cooked Seafood* when adding cream

*Raw shrimp or lobster: Sauté 2 cups seafood in butter at the beginning with 1 tsp Old Bay, remove and add back when adding cream and follow recipe for Basic Corn Chowder.

LENTIL, TOMATO & EGGPLANT SOUP

YIELDS: 2 1/2 QUARTS

THIS SOUP PAIRS GREAT WITH HUMMUS AND WARM PITA BREAD.

FOR A GREAT VEGETARIAN DINNER:
Ladle soup over cooked quinoa, rice or couscous and sprinkle with feta cheese.

1/4 cup	Canola Oil
2 cups	Eggplant, peeled and diced
1/2 cup	Onion, diced
1 tsp	Garlic, minced
1/2 tsp	Ginger - fresh, minced
2 tsp	Paprika
1/2 tsp	Cinnamon
1 tsp	Black Pepper
1 tsp	Kosher Salt
1 can (6 oz)	Tomato Paste
1/2 cup	Yellow Pepper
1/2 cup	Red Pepper
1 can (14.5 oz)	Fire Roasted Tomatoes
8 oz	Lentils, rinsed and drained
2 quarts	Vegetable Stock *(page 131)*

- Heat a soup pot over medium-high heat and add canola oil
- Add the onion and garlic, sauté until onion begins to sweat
- Add spices, cook 2 minutes to bloom
- Add eggplant* and sauté until eggplant starts to sweat
- Add peppers, lentils and tomatoes
- Add vegetable stock
- Bring to a boil, reduce heat, simmer until lentils are soft
- Adjust seasoning to taste with salt and pepper

*If eggplant is bitter, add a touch of sugar or agave nectar to balance the bitterness.

Lentils

Rich in numerous essential nutrients, high in dietary fiber and
IS THE 2ND HIGHEST RATIO OF PROTEIN FROM LEGUMES (AFTER SOYBEANS)
— approximately 12 grams per 1/4 cup serving.

Feta Salad

SERVES: 3 TO 4 PEOPLE

1 cup	Cucumbers, stripped with a peeler, cut in half, seeds removed, and bias sliced 1/2 inch wide
1 cup	Tomatoes *(best flavor)*, large diced, or cherry tomatoes cut in half
1/2 cup	Artichokes *(canned is okay)*, halved, or quartered if large
1/4 cup	Red Onion, thin julienne
1/4 cup	Feta, 3/4-inch cubed or crumbled
2 Tbsp	Flat Leaf Parsley, chopped
1 Tbsp	Oregano - fresh *(only use fresh)*
2 Tbsp	Olive Oil
1/2	Lemon, juiced
To taste	Kosher Salt and Black Pepper

- Toss vegetables together with a pinch of salt and fresh ground pepper
- Drizzle with olive oil and lemon juice
- **Optional:** Add 1/4 cup pitted kalamata olives

FOR A PARTY:
Arrange the ingredients on a platter, sprinkle with herbs and drizzle the olive oil and lemon juice on top.

Simple Hummus

YIELDS: 2 1/2 CUPS

2 cans (15 oz)	Chickpeas, drained
2 cloves	Garlic, chopped
1 1/2 tsp	Kosher Salt
1/3 cup	Tahini Paste
4 Tbsp	Lemon Juice, fresh squeezed
1/4 cup	Olive Oil
1/4 tsp	Cayenne Pepper

- Use a food processor, blend chickpeas, chopped garlic and salt for about 20–30 seconds
- Add tahini paste, cayenne pepper and lemon juice, slowly drizzle in olive oil while blending for about 20 seconds
- Add additional lemon or salt to taste

NOTE: Blend longer for a smoother consistency.
Add 1–2 Tbsp water for a light, airy consistency.

OYSTERS ROCKEFELLER BISQUE

YIELDS: 1 QUART *(3 TO 4 SERVINGS)*

2 Tbsp	Butter
1/4 cup	Red Onion, minced
1/4 cup	Celery, minced
1/2 cup	Fennel, minced
1/4 tsp	Black Pepper
2 Tbsp	Flour
1	Bay Leaf
1 cup	Dry White Wine, not sweet
1 cup	Fish Stock or Clam Juice
1 cup	Heavy Cream
1/4 cup	Red Pepper, minced
1 quart	Baby Spinach
1 tin	Shucked Oysters *(or 12-16 whole fresh Oysters, opened)*
1 tsp	Tabasco

- Heat a saucepan over medium heat
- Add butter, onions, celery and fennel, sauté until vegetables begin to sweat
- Add bay leaf and black pepper
- Continue cooking until vegetables are soft
- Sprinkle and blend in flour, cook for 3 minutes
- Slowly add wine, blend with vegetable mixture, then add fish stock or clam juice, bring to a boil, reduce heat and simmer for 4 minutes
- Add cream, simmer 3 minutes
- Add red pepper and spinach, cook until spinach wilts
- Add oysters, cook for 3-5 minutes or until oysters are cooked through
- Remove from heat, add tabasco
- Season to taste with salt and pepper

A crisp white wine & citrus salad will pair perfectly with this decadent soup.

* Puffed pastry cheese straws would be a great addition along with a simple dessert of baked apples.

Grapefruit & Red Onion Salad

SERVES: 2 TO 3 PEOPLE

1	Grapefruit, peeled and segmented
2 Tbsp	Red Onion, fine julienne
2 cups	Bibb Lettuce*, 1-inch pieces
4 Tbsp	Tangy Orange Dressing *(page 134)*

- Toss together
- **Optional:** Sprinkle salad with toasted nuts; add avocado

*I like the tender, sweet leaves of Bibb lettuce, but you can substitute field greens, baby spinach, arugula, baby kale, or watercress.

Cheese Straws

YIELDS: 10 TO 12 PIECES

FROM MY CATERING DAYS,

Cheese Straws were perfect to make ahead of time. I would freeze them and then bake for instant and delicious hors d'oeuvres.

1 sheet	Puffed pastry
1	Egg
1/4 cup	Water
1/2 cup	Shredded Parmesan Cheese *(or Italian Cheese Blend)*

- Preheat oven to 350°F
- Make egg wash by whisking egg and water together
- Place dough on a cutting board, brush with egg wash, then sprinkle cheese evenly on top
- Press the cheese into the dough with hands or rolling pin
- Cut dough into 3/4-inch strips, twist strips by holding the ends with fingers and turning in opposite directions *(to look like a corkscrew)*
- Place twists on a baking sheet, top with any cheese that has fallen off
- Bake for 18–20 minutes, until straws have puffed and are golden brown and flaky
- Let rest for at least 5-6 minutes before serving

BLACK BEAN & CHORIZO SAUSAGE SOUP

YIELDS: 3 QUARTS

1 Tbsp	Canola Oil
2 cups	Chorizo (9 oz), cooked, half-moon slices
1/2 cup	Onion, small diced
1/4 cup	Celery, small diced
1/4 cup	Red Bell Pepper, small diced
1/4 cup	Yellow Pepper, small diced
1/4 cup	Poblano Pepper, small diced
1 cup	Green Cabbage, thin julienne
2 cans (15 oz)	Black Beans, drained and rinsed
1 can (10 oz)	Rojo Tomatoes, medium heat
1 1/2 quarts	Chicken Stock *(page 130)*
1 tsp	Chipotle in Adobo, pureed
1/2 tsp	Kosher Salt
1/2 tsp	Black Pepper
1 Tbsp	Cornstarch, blended with 1/4 cup water
1/4 bunch	Cilantro, chopped
2 tsp	Lime Juice - fresh

- Heat soup pot over medium-high heat
- Add canola oil and chorizo sausage, sauté until sausage begins to brown
- Add onions and celery, cook until they start to sweat
- Add peppers, cabbage and chipotle in adobo
- Sauté until peppers begin to sweat, add tomatoes, black beans and chicken stock
- Bring to a boil, reduce heat, simmer for 15-20 minutes
- Add cornstarch, cilantro, lime juice, and salt and pepper
- Simmer for 5 minutes
- Adjust seasoning to taste with salt and pepper
- Serve each bowl with a wedge of lime

Avocado Tomato Salad

SERVES: 2 TO 4 PEOPLE

3 cups	Baby Spinach or Field Greens
2	Avocados, large diced
1 cup	Tomatoes, large diced, or Cherry Tomatoes, halved
1/4 cup	Sweet Onion, thin julienne

DRESSING:

1	Lime, juiced
1	Lemon, juiced
1/4 tsp	Chipotle in Adobo, pureed
2 tsp	Honey
1/4 tsp	Kosher Salt
2-3 Tbsp	Olive Oil

- Whisk dressing ingredients together in a large bowl
- Add spinach, tomatoes and onions
- Toss with dressing
- Add avocado and gently toss

Quick & Easy Chicken Wrap

SERVES: 4 TO 6 PEOPLE

4	Flour Tortillas
2	Avocados, smashed *(or 1 cup Guacamole)*
4	Lettuce Leaves
1 cup	Chicken, pulled *(use leftover rotisserie chicken)*
1 cup	Corn Salsa *(page 75)* or substitute your favorite salsa

- Lightly warm tortillas on a griddle pan or microwave for 20–30 seconds to make them pliable
- Place tortillas on a cutting board
- Spread entire tortilla with smashed avocado and sprinkle with kosher salt and pepper
- Top with lettuce leaf 3/4 way across tortilla
- Arrange chicken on top of lettuce
- Spoon salsa on top of chicken
- Roll wrap toward the last 1/4 *— the guacamole will hold the tortilla together*
- Cut in half on a slight bias
- **Optional:** Add pepper jack or cheddar cheese

Lemon Lime Ice {Granita}

YIELDS: 1 QUART

1 cup	Lemon Juice, fresh squeezed
1 cup	Lime Juice, fresh squeezed
2 cups	Water
2 cups	Sugar, granulated
2 tsp	Mint - fresh, fine julienne

- In a saucepan, combine all ingredients
- Over medium heat, bring to a boil, reduce heat, simmer for 2–3 minutes
- Remove from heat and let cool
- Place in 8-inch square baking pan *(metal)* and place in the freezer
- Freeze for 3–4 hours
- Scoop or flake with a fork
- Scoop in dishes
- Top with berries and fresh mint

CURRIED ZUCCHINI SOUP

YIELDS: 2 QUARTS

THIS SOUP IS PERFECT TO SERVE COLD IN THE SUMMER WHEN THE GARDEN IS OVERFLOWING WITH SQUASH.

* Top it with a dollop of plain yogurt blended with a touch of honey, squeeze of lime and mint.

1/4 cup	Canola Oil
1/2 cup	Onion, diced
1/2 cup	Celery, sliced
1 quart	Zucchini, large diced
1/2 tsp	Garlic, minced
1 Tbsp	Curry Powder
1/4 tsp	Cinnamon - ground
1/4 tsp	Cayenne Pepper
1 tsp	Kosher Salt
1/4 tsp	Ginger
1/4 tsp	Paprika
3 Tbsp	Flour
2 cans (14.5 oz)	Coconut Milk
1 1/2 cups	Apple Cider
1 cup	Water
4 tsp	Honey
1/2 cup	Apple, small diced
1/2 cup	Zucchini, small diced

- Heat soup pot over medium-high heat and add canola oil
- Add onion, celery, garlic and zucchini and sauté until vegetables begin to sweat
- Add spices and cook for 2 minutes to bloom
- Sprinkle with flour and cook for 4-5 minutes
- Add coconut milk, apple cider and water and blend thoroughly with vegetable mixture
- Bring to a boil, reduce heat and let simmer until vegetables are soft
- Puree with immersion blender until smooth
- Fold in apples and zucchini
- Add honey and let simmer about 5 minutes
- Add salt and pepper to taste

NOTE: If freezing, add 1 Tbsp cornstarch blended with 1/4 cup water with the honey. This helps stop cream from separating when reheating.

Summer Berry Salad

SERVES: 2 TO 3 PEOPLE

2 cups	Greens — Field Greens, Julienne Kale, Baby Spinach, Arugula
1/2 cup	Fresh Berries — Blackberries, Strawberries, Blueberries, Raspberries
1 Tbsp	Green Onions, thin circle slices
2 Tbsp	Nuts — Toasted or Candied Almonds, Cashews, Pecans *(page 140)*
3 Tbsp	Dressing — Pomegranate, Tangy Orange, Balsamic or Champagne Vinaigrette *(pages 134 & 135)*
2 Tbsp	Goat, Blue or Feta Cheese *(optional)*

- In a bowl, toss the lettuce, green onions, berries and dressing together
- Sprinkle with nuts and optional cheese

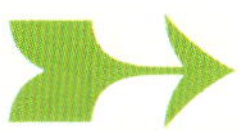

SUGGESTED PAIRING:

Drizzle naan bread with a little olive oil and warm on a griddle or grill pan.

RANCH STEAK SOUP

YIELDS: 2 QUARTS

NEXT TIME YOU ARE GRILLING, ADD SOME EXTRA VEGETABLES TO THE GRILL AND SAVE THEM FOR THIS SOUP.

The addition of grilled peppers, onions and corn brings the flavor profile to a whole new level.

1/4 cup	Canola Oil
10 oz	Steak* *(Top Sirloin or Tri-tip)*
1 1/2 cups	Onions, julienne
2 tsp	Garlic, minced
1/2 tsp	Chipotle Powder
1 1/2 cups	Baby Red Potatoes, half-moon slices
1 cup	Red Pepper, julienne
1/2 cup	Yellow Pepper, julienne
1/2 cup	Poblano Pepper, julienne
1 Tbsp	Jalapeños, minced
1 cup	Corn
2 quarts	Beef Stock *(page 130)*
1/2 cup	Barbecue Sauce
2	Bay Leaves
2 Tbsp	Cilantro
2 Tbsp	Cornstarch, blended with 1/4 cup water

- Heat a soup pot over medium-high heat with canola oil
- Sauté steak for 2-4 minutes on each side, remove from heat and let rest**
- Add onions, garlic, potatoes, chipotle powder and salt
- Sauté until onions begin to sweat and potatoes start to brown
- Add bay leaves, peppers and jalapeños and cook for 4 minutes
- Add beef stock, barbecue sauce and corn
- Bring to a boil, then reduce heat and simmer until vegetables are soft
- Add cilantro and cornstarch, simmer 3 minutes
- Adjust seasoning with salt and pepper to taste
- Cut steak in half lengthwise, then slice on a bias and add to soup

*Substitute chicken for steak.
** Optional: omit the step and used leftover grilled steak or chicken.

Dropped Cheese Biscuits

YIELDS: 12 BISCUITS

2 1/4 cups	Flour
2 1/2 tsp	Baking Powder
2 tsp	Sugar
3/4 tsp	Baking Soda
1 tsp	Salt
6 Tbsp	Butter, cold and diced
1 cup	Cheddar Cheese, grated
1/2 cup	Pepper Jack Cheese, grated
1 cup	Buttermilk

- Preheat oven to 425°F
- In a bowl, whisk all dry ingredients
- Add butter and with fingers blend with dry ingredients until it resembles coarse meal
- Fold in the grated cheeses
- Add buttermilk, stir just until everything is combined *(do not overmix)*
- Using a large soupspoon, drop 12 even-size biscuits on a parchment-lined or greased baking tray
- Lightly brush tops with buttermilk
- Bake for approximately 18–20 minutes, until golden brown on top and bottom
- **Optional:** Add green onions or chives with the cheese

Summer Tomato Salad

SERVES: 4 TO 6 PEOPLE

3	Tomatoes*, cored and sliced
2 tsp	Sweet Onion, finely minced or grated
1/2 tsp	Garlic, finely minced or grated
1 Tbsp	Red Wine Vinegar
2 Tbsp	Olive Oil
To taste	Salt and Black Pepper

- Sprinkle the sliced tomatoes with salt and pepper *(seasoning tomato with salt brings out the natural flavor)*
- Mix the onion, garlic, vinegar and oil, and spoon over tomatoes
- Let marinate for at least 10 minutes
- **Optional:** Top with grated ricotta salata and/or basil chiffonade

*I like to use a colorful variety of tomatoes for a contrast of flavor, texture and color, but any ripe tomato is fine. If the skin is tough, peel with a very sharp knife before slicing.

CLASSIC TOMATO SOUP

YIELDS: 3 QUARTS

THE PERFECT PAIR:

Tomato Soup and Grilled Cheese Sandwich

1/4 cup	Olive Oil
1 cup	Onions, diced
1/2 cup	Celery, diced
1 cup	Carrots, diced
1 Tbsp	Garlic, minced
1 tsp	Black Pepper
2	Bay Leaves
2 cans (28 oz)	San Marzano Tomatoes
1/2 cup	Brown Sugar
1 quart	Vegetable Stock *(page 131)*
1	Lemon, zest
2 Tbsp	Red Wine Vinegar
2 Tbsp	Cornstarch, blended with 1/4 cup water
1 pint	Heavy Cream*

- Heat a soup pot over medium-high heat
- Add olive oil, onions, carrots, celery and garlic, sauté until the vegetables sweat and onions begin to turn translucent
- Add pepper, bay leaves, tomatoes, brown sugar, stock and vinegar
- Bring to a boil, reduce heat and slowly simmer for 45 minutes to 1 hour
- Puree soup with an immersion blender
- Add cornstarch and lemon zest
- Simmer for another 3-5 minutes
- Taste and add salt and pepper if needed
- Finish with cream and simmer for 3-5 additional minutes

*Make it vegan and omit the cream and replace with either additional stock or almond or soy milk.

Grilled Cheese Sandwich

SERVES: 1 PER PERSON

- Heat griddle to medium heat
- Place 3 to 4 slices of your favorite cheese between 2 slices of bread
- Lightly butter outside of each bread slice
- Grill until golden brown, flip and brown other side, approximately 3 minutes per side
- **Optional additions:** tomato, bacon, ham, apple, caramelized onions and/or pineapple

FOR A FUN TWIST...

Pepper Jelly Grilled Cheese Sandwich

- Lay out 2 slices of bread
- On one slice of bread, spread 1 Tbsp cream cheese on one side, then top with 1 Tbsp pepper jelly and 2 slices of cheddar cheese
- Top with the remaining slice and butter outside of each bread slice
- Grill until golden brown, flip, and brown other side, approximately 3 minutes per side

Monster Cookies

YIELDS: 16 TO 24 COOKIES

1 roll Chocolate Chip Cookie Dough* — favorite store-bought brand
1/2 bag Mini M&M's® milk chocolate baking bits
(or substitute with traditional size)

- Cut the cookies into the portion size you want
- Lightly press each portion into the M&M's, covering all sides
- Follow baking instructions on the cookie dough package, remove from oven and let cool
- Discard any leftover M&M's that were used to roll the cookies in

*If making the chocolate chip cookie dough from scratch, chill at least 30 minutes before rolling in M&M's.

Peanut Butter Cup Cookies

YIELDS: 24 COOKIES

My sister started making these for a quick special twist when her boys were in school. Now, at Christmas, these simple cookies are still THE FIRST TO GO!

Chocolate Chip Cookie Dough* — favorite store-bought brand
(substitute Peanut Butter Dough)
1 bag Mini Reese's® Peanut Butter Cups

- Half fill mini muffin cups with chocolate chip cookie dough
- Follow baking instructions on the cookie dough package
- Remove from oven 2 minutes early, place a peanut butter cup in center of each cookie and lightly press into the dough
- Return to oven, bake for 1–2 additional minutes, then remove from oven and cool

*If making the chocolate chip cookie dough from scratch, chill at least 30 minutes.

THAI COCONUT SOUP

YIELDS: 3 QUARTS

1/4 cup	Canola Oil
8 oz	Chicken Breast, raw
1/2 tsp	Kosher Salt
1/4 tsp	Black Pepper
1/4 cup	Ginger, minced
1/2 cup	Shiitake Mushrooms *(substitute Button)*
1/2 cup	Onions, thin julienne
1/2 cup	Red Pepper, 1/2-inch long strips
1/4 cup	Carrots, shredded
1 cup	Bok Choy*, 1/2-inch wide strips
2 Tbsp	Red Curry Paste
1 stick	Lemon Grass
1 tsp	Kaffir Lime Leaves
1 can (14 oz)	Coconut Milk
2 quarts	Chicken Stock *(page 130)*
3 Tbsp	Cornstarch, blended with 1/4 cup water
2 tsp	Fish Sauce
1 tsp	Lime Zest
1/4 cup	Cilantro, chopped

- Cut chicken breast on a thin bias slice and sprinkle with salt and pepper
- Heat a soup pot over medium-high heat with canola oil
- Quickly sauté chicken, remove from pan, set aside to add back in later
- Add onions, ginger and lemon grass, begin to sauté
- Add shiitake mushrooms and sauté until they begin to sweat
- Add red curry paste, bok choy and kaffir lime leaves
- Add chicken stock and coconut milk
- Bring to a boil, add carrots, red pepper, and cooked chicken
- Reduce heat and simmer for 10–12 minutes
- Add cornstarch, fish sauce, cilantro and lime
- Simmer for 5 minutes
- Adjust seasoning with salt and pepper to taste
- Serve each bowl with a wedge of lime
- **Optional:** For a fun twist, add or substitute shrimp for chicken

*Substitute napa cabbage for bok choy.

MAKE IT AN ASIAN BOWL:

- Place cooked rice stick noodles, jasmine or brown rice in the bottom of a bowl
- Ladle soup over the rice and top with fresh cilantro or basil leaves

Cashew Pineapple Salad

SERVES: 3 TO 4 PEOPLE

1 head	Bibb Lettuce, torn into bite-size pieces
2 oz	Rice Wine Vinegar
1 Tbsp	Honey
1/2 tsp	Sriracha Sauce *(optional)*
1/2	Lime, juiced
1/4	Pineapple, small diced
1	Orange, cored, peeled and diced
1/4 cup	Coconut, toasted
1/4 cup	Curried Cashews *(page 141)*

- In a mixing bowl, whisk the rice wine vinegar, honey, lime juice and sriracha sauce
- Add the Bibb lettuce and toss
- Add the rest of the ingredients and toss
- Optional: Place the tossed lettuce on a platter and arrange the rest of the ingredients on top

Mango Ginger Cream

SERVES: 2 TO 4 PEOPLE

1 cup	Mango*, pureed
2 Tbsp	Agave Nectar
1 tsp	Crystallized Ginger, minced
1	Lime, zest and juice
1 cup	Greek Yogurt — Plain, Coconut or Vanilla
1/4 cup	Toasted Coconut
2 Tbsp	Nutty Granola *(page 97)*

- Puree mango, mix with ginger, agave, and marinate for 15 minutes
- Add yogurt and toasted coconut, fold together
- Spoon into dishes, top with Nutty Granola

**Substitute berries, peaches, bananas or pears.*

THANKSGIVING TURKEY SOUP

YIELDS: 4 QUARTS

EVERYBODY'S THANKSGIVING FEAST IS A LITTLE DIFFERENT.

THIS SOUP SHOULD HAVE A UNIQUE TWIST UTILIZING YOUR LEFTOVERS. Use this basic recipe as a starting point and be creative. For example, whisking in leftover mashed or sweet potatoes is a great way to thicken the soup. Small pieces of stuffing can create little dumplings instead of using noodles or rice.

Turkey Stock

- Remove the meat from the carcass and place carcass in a large pot, also scrape any drippings from the pan into the pot
- Add 1 onion, 1-2 carrots, 1-2 ribs of celery, sprigs/stems from the leftover herbs, sage, thyme, parsley, rosemary and 2 bay leaves
- Cover with water 2 inches above the carcass, bring to a boil, reduce heat, and simmer until the liquid is reduced by approximately half
- Strain and cool
- Chill overnight and remove the congealed fat from the top of the stock

Don't have time to make stock? Remove the meat from the bones, add the drippings from the bottom of the pan and freeze for another day.

TURKEY SOUP

1/4 cup	Canola Oil
1 cup	Onions, diced
1/2 cup	Celery, straight cut
1 cup	Carrots, circle cut
1 tsp	Garlic, minced
1 cup	Mushrooms, sliced
1 can (14 oz)	Tomatoes, diced
1/2 cup	Corn
2 tsp	Sage - fresh
3 quarts	Turkey Stock *(see stock recipe above)*
1 cups	Egg Noodles *(substitute Rice or Barley)*
2 Tbsp	Parsley, chopped
1 1/2 cups	Turkey *(optional)*

- Heat a soup pot over medium-high heat with canola oil
- Add onions, garlic and celery, sauté until they begin to sweat
- Add carrots, mushrooms and herbs, cook for 3 minutes
- Add tomatoes, corn and turkey stock, bring to a boil, reduce heat, simmer for 15 minutes
- Add noodles, cook until al dente
- Add parsley and turkey
- Adjust seasoning to taste with salt and pepper

NOTE: If freezing, cook pasta separately and fold into soup once cold before packaging in containers.

TURKEY POSOLE

YIELDS: 2 1/2 QUARTS

POSOLE MEANS HOMINY AND IS A TRADITIONAL MEXICAN SOUP USUALLY MADE WITH PORK.

I find this soup another great way to use leftover Thanksgiving turkey. With the flavor profile so different from traditional Thanksgiving flavors, nobody knows they are eating leftovers!

1/4 cup	Canola Oil
1 cup	Onions, diced
1/2 cup	Carrots, diced
2 tsp	Garlic, minced
1 Tbsp	Chili Powder
1 1/2 tsp	Cumin
1 1/2 tsp	Smoked Paprika
1/2 tsp	Black Pepper
1 tsp	Kosher Salt
1 1/2 tsp	Oregano
3 Tbsp	Tomato Paste
1 can (10 oz)	Diced Tomatoes with Green Chilies
1 1/2 quarts	Southwest Turkey Stock *(see stock recipe below)*
1 can (25 oz)	Hominy, drained and rinsed
2 cups	Turkey*, pulled
2 Tbsp	Lime Juice - fresh

- Heat soup pot to medium-high heat with canola oil
- Add onions, garlic and carrots and sauté until the vegetables begin to sweat
- Add spices and sauté for 2 minutes to bloom the spices
- Add the tomato paste and cook 1 minute
- Add tomatoes, hominy and turkey stock, bring to a boil, reduce heat, simmer 20–25 minutes
- Add salt and pepper to taste
- Add pulled turkey and simmer 4 minutes

*No Turkey? Substitute chicken stock and pulled rotisserie chicken.

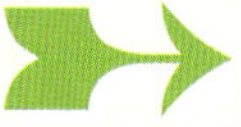

ADD YOUR OWN UNIQUE TWIST:

TRY DIFFERENT TOPPINGS LIKE SHREDDED CABBAGE, CILANTRO LEAVES, SHAVED JALAPEÑO, SHAVED RADISHES, DICED AVOCADO OR TORTILLA CHIPS!

Southwest Turkey Stock

- **KICK UP THE TURKEY STOCK WITH SOUTHWEST FLAVORS:** Add garlic, cilantro stems, smashed jalepeños or dried chilies from your pantry.

CREAM OF CAULIFLOWER

YIELDS: 1 1/2 QUARTS

1 1/2 lb	Cauliflower, chopped
1 cup	Onion, diced
4 Tbsp	Butter
4 Tbsp	Flour
6 cups	Milk
1/4 tsp	Nutmeg, ground
1 tsp	Kosher Salt
1/2 tsp	Black Pepper

GARNISH:**

1/2 cup	Cauliflower Florets
1/4 cup	Red Pepper, small diced

- Heat a soup pot on medium-high heat
- Add butter, onions and cauliflower, sauté until vegetables begin to sweat
- Sprinkle and blend flour over vegetable mixture, cook for 5 minutes, stirring often to prevent burning on the bottom of the pot
- Slowly add in the milk and stir well
- Bring to a boil, reduce heat, simmer 15–20 minutes, stirring often
- Blend with immersion blender until smooth
- Add the nutmeg, salt and pepper to taste
- Fold in garnish cauliflower and red pepper
- Simmer for 3–4 minutes

NOTE: If freezing, add 1 Tbsp cornstarch blended with 1/4 cup water with garnish vegetables. This helps stop cream from separating during reheating process.

Chicken or Vegetable Stock *(page 130)* **can be substituted for the milk, finish with 1/2 cup of heavy cream or almond milk to add a RICH, CREAMY TEXTURE.**

Classic Spinach Salad

SERVES: 4 TO 6 PEOPLE

5 cups	Baby Spinach
10	Pear Tomatoes, split in half
2	Hard-Boiled Eggs
1 cup	Mushrooms, thinly sliced
1/2 cup	Red or Sweet Onions, shaved
8 slices	Bacon*, cooked and julienne
4 oz	Dressing — Warm Bacon Dressing *(page 135)* or Honey Mustard Vinaigrette *(page 134)*

- Toss spinach, onions, mushrooms and dressing
- Place in serving bowl, arrange bacon, tomatoes and sliced eggs on top
- **Optional:** Add 1/4 cup blue or goat cheese

*A quality applewood or hickory smoked bacon brings the best flavor.

Simple Apple Fruit Tart

YIELDS: 6 TO 10 PIECES

THIS DELICIOUS DESSERT IS GREAT FOR ENTERTAINING.

It looks fancy but is really simple and easy.

1 sheet	Puffed Pastry
2	Apples, thinly sliced *(1/8 to 1/4 inch)*
2 tsp	Cinnamon - ground
3/4 cup	Sugar

- Preheat oven to 385°F
- In a small bowl, mix cinnamon and sugar
- Cut the puffed pastry into squares 1/8 inch larger than the width of the apple slices
- Place puffed pastry on a sheet pan
- With a fork, dock the puffed pastry *(poke holes around the dough to stop it from rising)*
- Toss the apples in half the cinnamon sugar
- Arrange the apple slices slightly touching across the puffed pastry
- Sprinkle apple slices with remaining cinnamon sugar
- Bake for 15 to 18 minutes
- Pastry will be a nice golden brown on the bottom and apples will be soft
- Cool for about 5 minutes, then sprinkle with powdered sugar

OPTIONS:

- Great with ice cream
- Substitute other fruits for apples — peaches, plums, apricots or grapes

PULLED BUFFALO CHICKEN SOUP

YIELDS: 2 1/2 QUARTS

SERVE THIS SOUP WITH A SIMPLE GARDEN SALAD
with Buttermilk Ranch or 1000 Island Dressing *(page 135)*.

1/4 cup	Canola Oil
1 cup	Celery, large diced
1 cup	Carrots, large diced
3/4 cup	Onion, large diced
1 1/2 cups	Yukon Gold Potatoes, peeled and cubed
3 Tbsp	Flour
1/2 cup	Buffalo Wing Hot Sauce
2	Bay Leaves
2 quarts	Chicken Stock *(page 130)*
1	Hidden Valley® Buttermilk Ranch, dry packet
1/2 tsp	Kosher Salt
1/2 tsp	Black Pepper

GARNISH TO SIMMER IN SOUP:

3/4 cup	Celery, thin bias sliced including leaves
3/4 cup	Carrots, thin circle cut
1/2 cup	Green Onions, thin circle cut
2 Tbsp	Cornstarch, blended with 1/4 cup water
2 cups	Pulled Chicken
2 Tbsp	Buffalo Wing Hot Sauce

- Heat a soup pot over medium-high heat with canola oil
- Sauté onions, carrots and celery until the vegetables begin to sweat
- Add potatoes, bay leaves and flour
- Cook for 3 minutes
- Add buffalo wing hot sauce, ranch dressing packet and chicken stock
- Bring to a boil, reduce heat, simmer until potatoes are soft
- Puree with immersion blender
- Add the garnish vegetables
- Simmer for 5 minutes
- Season to taste with salt and pepper
- Add cornstarch and cook for 5 minutes
- Toss chicken in hot sauce and add to individual bowls when serving

TO SERVE:

- Toss the pulled chicken in hot sauce
- Ladle soup into bowls
- Top each bowl with pulled chicken
- For a spicier version, drizzle hot sauce on top of each bowl
- Serve a Mini Blue & Cheddar Cheese Sandwich *(page 49)* on top or on the side

Mini Blue & Cheddar Cheese Sandwiches

YIELDS: 6 TO 8 SANDWICHES

BREAD:

1	Baguette*
1 Tbsp	Butter, softened

CHEESE SPREAD:

GREAT SPREAD FOR HOLIDAY ENTERTAINING OR WITH HAM OR TURKEY SANDWICHES!

- Roll in chopped Toasted Pecans or Walnuts and serve with crackers, bread or apple slices.

BLEND TOGETHER:

2/3 cup	Sharp Cheddar shredded
1/3 cup	Crumbled Blue Cheese
1/4 cup	Mayonnaise
1/4 cup	Green Apple, minced
2 tsp	Green Onion, thin circle cut
1/8 tsp	Black Pepper
1/8 tsp	Kosher Salt

ASSEMBLY:

- Slice baguette on a bias, stack in twos on a cutting board
- Spread 1 Tbsp of the cheese filling on the top slice and top with remaining slice
- Lightly butter the outside of each slice
- Griddle sandwich over medium heat until golden brown, flip and brown the other side

*Substitute pretzel or rye bread for baguette.

Pulled Buffalo Chicken Soup

SPLIT PEA & HAM SOUP

YIELDS: 2 QUARTS

1/4 cup	Canola Oil
1 cup	Ham, diced
1 cup	Onion, diced
1 tsp	Garlic, chopped
1	Medium Baking Potato, peeled and diced
1 lb	Split Peas, rinsed and drained
2 quarts	Chicken Stock *(page 130)*
2	Bay Leaves
1 cup	Carrots, shredded
1/2 tsp	Kosher Salt
1 tsp	Tabasco

- Heat soup pot over medium heat
- Add canola oil, sauté ham
- Remove 1/3 of the ham from pan to add back later for garnish
- Add onions and garlic, sauté until onions begin to sweat
- Add split peas, potatoes and bay leaves
- Add chicken stock, bring to a boil, reduce heat, simmer until the split peas are tender
- Puree with immersion blender until smooth
  — if thick, add stock or water to desired consistency
- Add salt, Tabasco, shredded carrots, and ham
- Simmer for 8–10 minutes
- Adjust seasoning to taste with salt and pepper

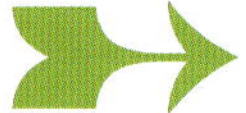

TO KICK UP THE FLAVOR:

Add a leftover ham bone or ham hock* when adding the potato and split peas with 1 quart of water and 1 quart chicken stock.

*If you don't eat pork, substitute smoked turkey legs for the ham.

There was a restaurant in Vienna, Virginia, that served
a delicious split pea soup & a salad with mandarin oranges.
I had many wonderful lunches eating soup,
drinking white wine and laughing with friends!

I USE THIS MANDARIN ORANGE ALMOND SALAD AS A QUICK, EASY & TASTY WAY TO SPARK UP A SIMPLE MEAL.

Mandarin Orange Almond Salad

SERVES: 2 TO 3 PEOPLE

TOSS TOGETHER:

2 cups	Romaine Lettuce
1/2 can	Mandarin Oranges or 1 Clementine
2 Tbsp	Smoked Almonds
2 tsp	Red Peppers, small diced

DRESSING:

3 Tbsp	Red Wine Vinaigrette*
2 Tbsp	Blue Cheese Crumbles *(optional)*

*Substitute Honey Mustard or Pomegranate Vinaigrette *(page 134)*.

Gingerbread

YIELDS: 1 PAN

The aromas of soup simmering on the stove and fresh gingerbread baking in the oven sets the stage for a PERFECT EVENING MEAL ON A CHILLY FALL DAY.

FOR A FUN TWIST:

Make cupcakes and top with a lemon buttercream.

1 cup	Canola Oil
1 cup	Sugar
1 cup	Molasses
2 Tbsp	Crystallized Ginger, minced
2	Eggs
3 cups	Flour
1 Tbsp	Ginger, ground
2 tsp	Cinnamon, ground
1 tsp	Salt
1/4 tsp	Cloves, ground
1/4 tsp	Nutmeg
1 cup	Water, boiling
1 Tbsp	Baking Soda

- Preheat oven to 325°F
- Spray/lightly butter a 9x13-inch baking pan
- Whisk canola oil, sugar, molasses, crystallized ginger and eggs together until smooth
- In another bowl, whisk the dry ingredients together
- Whisk the dry mixture into the molasses mixture
- Stir the baking soda into the boiling water, then whisk into the batter
- Pour into baking pan and bake for approximately 45 minutes or until a toothpick comes out clean
- Cool and sprinkle with powder sugar

GARDEN VEGETABLE SOUP

YIELDS: 3 1/2 QUARTS

i call this my FREE SOUP!

- It's super low in calories and really fills you up.
- Ladle it over cooked quinoa or barley for added protein.

1/4 cup	Canola oil
1 cup	Onions, diced
1 cup	Baby Carrots, circle cut
1 tsp	Garlic, chopped
1/2 cup	Celery, 1/4-inch slices
1 can (14.5 oz)	Tomatoes, diced
1 cup	Zucchini, large diced
1 1/2 cups	Cabbage, 1-inch shred
6 cups	Kale, 3/4-inch pieces
2 sprigs	Thyme - fresh
2 tsp	Oregano - dry
2 Tbsp	Basil - fresh, chopped
2	Bay Leaves
1 1/2 tsp	Kosher Salt
1 tsp	Black Pepper
2 1/2 quarts	Vegetable Stock *(page 131)*
1/4 cup	Balsamic Vinegar
1 Tbsp	Cornstarch, blended with 1/4 cup water

- Heat a soup pot over medium-high heat
- Add canola oil, sauté onions, carrots, celery and garlic until they begin to sweat
- Add thyme, oregano, bay leaf, salt and pepper
- Add zucchini and cabbage, sauté until they begin to sweat
- Add balsamic vinegar, cook 2 minutes
- Add the tomatoes and vegetable stock
- Bring to a boil, reduce heat and simmer for 15 minutes
- Add the kale and continue to simmer for another 8–10 minutes
- Add salt and pepper to taste
- Add basil and cornstarch, simmer an additional 5 minutes

Grilled Turkey & Swiss Sandwich

SERVES: 1 TO 2 PEOPLE

As needed	Olive Oil or Butter
2 slices	Multigrain Bread
1 tsp	Dijon Mustard*
3 slices	Swiss Cheese *(1 1/2 slices per side)*
3 slices	Turkey
5 slices	Bread & Butter Pickles

- Heat a griddle pan or panini press to medium heat
- Spread a thin layer of Dijon mustard on the bottom slice of bread
- Top mustard with 1 1/2 slices of Swiss cheese, 3 slices of turkey, pickles, then the other 1 1/2 slices of Swiss cheese
- Top with the remaining slice of bread
- Lightly spread butter or oil on the outsides of the sandwich and on griddle or press
- Cook about 3–4 minutes
- Flip and cook the other side for approximately 3 minutes
- The cheese should be melted and sandwich a nice golden brown
- Let rest for 1 minute, then cut in half and serve

*Substitute 1000 Island Dressing (page 135) for mustard.

Chocolate Cherry Crumble

SERVES: 6 TO 8 PEOPLE

FILLING:

1 can (21 oz)	Cherry Pie Filling
1/2 tsp	Almond Extract
1 tsp	Cinnamon

CRUMBLE:

1/3 cup	Cocoa Powder
2/3 cup	Sugar, granulated
3/4 cup	Flour
1/2 tsp	Orange Zest
1 tsp	Cinnamon - ground
6 Tbsp	Butter, melted
1/4 cup	Chocolate Chips, dark or semisweet

- Preheat oven to 375°F
- Spray a 1 1/2 quart baking dish
- Mix the cherry pie filling, almond extract and cinnamon, place in the bottom of the baking dish
- In a bowl, toss all dry ingredients together, add melted butter, gently toss until mixture forms pea-size pieces, then fold in chocolate chips
- Sprinkle on top of filling
- Bake in oven for 25–30 minutes
- Filling should be bubbling through the browned crumble

ROASTED POBLANO & CORN BISQUE

YIELDS: 2 1/2 QUARTS

2 cups	Corn*
2	Poblano Peppers, roasted, seeds and skin removed
1/4 cup	Canola Oil
1/2 cup	Onions, diced
1 tsp	Garlic, chopped
3 Tbsp	Flour
1 1/4 quarts	Corn Stock *(page 55)* or Vegetable Stock *(page 131)*
8 oz	Cream Cheese

GARNISH:

1/2 cup	Red Peppers, small diced
1/4 cup	Poblano Peppers, small diced
1 cup	Corn
2 Tbsp	Cilantro, chopped
1/2 tsp	Salt
1/2 tsp	Black Pepper
1 Tbsp	Cornstarch, blended with 1/4 cup water

- Heat soup pot over medium heat with canola oil
- Add onions and garlic, sauté until onions begin to sweat
- Add corn and roasted poblano peppers, cook for 2–3 minutes
- Sprinkle and blend flour into the vegetable mixture to form a roux, then cook for 3 minutes
- Add vegetable stock slowly and blend together
- Bring to boil reduce heat and simmer for 10–12 minutes
- Dice cream cheese and add to soup
- Puree with immersion blender
- Add the garnish vegetables, salt and pepper, simmer for 5 minutes
- Adjust seasoning to taste with salt and pepper, then add cornstarch mixture.
- Simmer for 3 to 4 minutes
- Taste and add additional salt and pepper to taste

*It is best to use corn cut off the cob, but it is okay to substitute frozen corn.

How to Roast Poblano Peppers:

OPTION 1:

- Roast over an open flame or griddle pan, blackening the pepper on all sides
- Cool, remove skin and seeds

OPTION 2:

- Spray sheet pan and place peppers on sheet pan
- Roast in a 400°F oven for 10 minutes
- Turn the peppers over for even cooking, continue roasting until the outsides blacken and peppers are soft
- Cool, remove skin and seeds

Fresh Corn Stock

YIELDS: 1 1/4 QUARTS

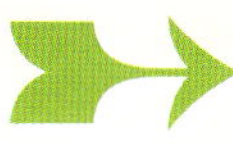

A GREAT WAY TO ADD DEPTH OF CORN FLAVOR TO THIS SOUP!

- After corn is removed, take the cobs and toss with 2 Tbsp oil
- Roast cobs for 15 minutes in a 375°F oven
- Place in a soup pot, cover with 2 1/2 quarts of water
- Bring to a boil, reduce heat, and slowly simmer until liquid is reduced by half
- Remove cobs from stock

Pulled BBQ Chicken Salad Sliders

YIELDS: 12 EACH

SALAD:

2 cups	Rotisserie Chicken, pulled
1/4 cup	Barbecue Sauce
1/4 cup	Mayonnaise
1/3 cup	Celery, diced
1/4 cup	Red Onion, minced
1 Tbsp	Chopped Parsley or Cilantro

SLIDERS:

12	Mini Hawaiian Rolls
3 leaves	Lettuce, torn in quarters
12 sliced	Plum Tomatoes
12 slices	Bread & Butter Pickles

- Toss all salad ingredients together
- Season to taste with salt and pepper
- Split rolls, top with lettuce, tomato, pickle, then chicken salad

OPTIONAL:

- Add avocado or pickled onions
- Substitute Bibb lettuce for bread to make lettuce cups

CARROT FENNEL SOUP

YIELDS: 2 1/2 QUARTS

This soup is great all year long, but for me the color and flavors say Spring and Easter.

TRY IT COLD IN THE SUMMER FOR A LIGHT, REFRESHING DINNER.

1/4 cup	Canola oil
1 1/2 cups	Fennel *(approximately 1 bulb)*, washed and cut into 1/2-inch pieces
2 lb bag	Carrots, tops removed, washed and cut into 1-inch pieces
1 cup	Onions, large diced
2 tsp	Garlic, minced
2	Bay Leaves
1 tsp	Kosher Salt
1/2 tsp	Black Pepper
2 Tbsp	Flour
2 quarts	Water
2 Tbsp	Cornstarch, blended with 1/4 cup water
1 cup	Heavy Cream

- Heat a soup pot over medium-high heat with canola oil
- Add onions, fennel and garlic, sauté until the vegetables begin to sweat
- Add salt, pepper, bay leaves and flour, blend well
- Cook for 4 minutes
- Add carrots and water
- Bring to a boil, reduce heat and simmer until carrots are soft and ready to puree
- Puree mixture with an immersion blender
- Add cornstarch and heavy cream
- Simmer another 3–4 minutes
- Season to taste with salt and pepper
- Garnish with chopped fennel fronds, if available, or add 2 Tbsp finely chopped parsley

Chicken Fontina Melt

Chicken Fontina Melt

SERVES: 1 TO 2 PEOPLE

1	Ciabatta Roll
1 Tbsp	Lemon Mayo *(recipe below)*
1	Grilled Chicken Breast*, thin bias sliced
2 slices	Tomato *(or substitute Roasted Tomatoes)*
4	Asparagus Spears, blanched
2 slices	Fontina Cheese*

- Preheat oven to 350°F
- Split roll, open, spread both sides with lemon mayo
- Top bottom side with grilled chicken, tomato, salt, pepper, asparagus and fontina cheese
- Place sandwich on sheet pan and bake for 6-8 minutes or until the cheese begins to melt and bread gets crusty
- Remove and cut in half

*Substitute turkey for chicken or Havarti cheese for fontina.

Lemon Mayo

YIELDS: 1 CUP

GREAT FOR CHICKEN OR SHRIMP SALAD

BLEND TOGETHER:

1 cup	Mayonnaise
1	Lemon, zest from all, juice from half
1/4 tsp	Black Pepper

Strawberry Watercress Salad

SERVES: 3 TO 4 PEOPLE

1 bunch	Watercress, trim thick woody stems
1 cup	Strawberries, sliced
1/4 cup	Candied Nuts
	— Ginger Orange Almonds or Cashews *(page 141)*
4 Tbsp	Tangy Orange Dressing *(page 134)*

- Toss together
- **Optional:** Sprinkle with feta or goat cheese

CLASSIC MINESTRONE

YIELDS: 2 QUARTS

1/4 cup	Canola oil
3 oz	Pancetta, diced
1/2 cup	Onion
2 tsp	Garlic, minced
1/2 cup	Celery
1/2 cup	Carrots
1/2 cup	Zucchini
1 can (14 oz)	Tomatoes, diced
2 inch piece	Parmesan Cheese Rind
1 1/2 tsp	Oregano, dry whole leaf
1/2 tsp	Black Pepper
2	Bay Leaves
2 sprigs	Thyme - fresh
1/2 tsp	Kosher Salt
1/4 cup	Garbanzo Beans
1/4 cup	White Cannellini Beans
1 cup	Cabbage, shredded
1/2 cup	Pasta *(Ditalini or small Macaroni)*
2 quarts	Chicken Stock *(page 130)*
1 Tbsp	Cornstarch, blended with 1/4 cup water
1 Tbsp	Basil - fresh, chopped
1 Tbsp	Flat Leaf Parsley, chopped

- Heat a soup pot over medium-high heat
- Add Pancetta and cook until it begins to brown
- Add onions, garlic, celery and carrots, sauté until the vegetables start to sweat
- Add herbs, Parmesan rind, cabbage and zucchini, cook for 3–4 minutes
- Add tomatoes, beans and chicken stock
- Bring to a boil, add pasta, reduce heat, and simmer for 8 minutes
- Add the basil, parsley and cornstarch, simmer for 3 minutes
- Adjust seasoning to taste with salt and pepper
- When serving, top with fresh grated Parmesan cheese

Simple Hazelnut Mocha Sauce

Crusty Caesar Sandwiches

YIELDS: 3 TO 5 SANDWICHES

1	Baguette
2 cups	Romaine Lettuce
1/3 cup	Caesar Dressing *(page 135)*
1/4 cup	Shaved Parmesan
1/4 cup	Roasted Tomatoes
2	Grilled Chicken*, cut into thin slices on a slight bias
2 Tbsp	Shaved Parmesan, for topping

BREAD:

- Preheat oven to 375°F
- Split baguette in half and remove about half the inside of the bread
- Place on a sheet pan, bake for 5–6 minutes, until outside is crisp but center is soft

FILLING:

- Toss the romaine lettuce, Parmesan cheese, roasted tomatoes with Caesar dressing

BUILD SANDWICH:

- Fill the center of the bread with salad so it is slightly overflowing
- Top with chicken and sprinkle with Parmesan cheese
- Place top of bread, then lightly squeeze so bread nestles around the filling
- Cut into 2- to 3-inch pieces

*Substitute grilled steak, shrimp or salmon for chicken.

Simple Hazelnut Mocha Sauce

YIELDS: 1 1/2 CUPS

1 cup	Nutella®
1 cup	Coffee*, reduced to 1/2 cup
1	Orange, zest and juice

- Place the coffee in a small saucepan and reduce by half
- Add Nutella and orange, blend together
- Bring to a boil, remove from heat and cool at least 10 minutes
- Spoon over strawberries, bananas, oranges or your favorite ice cream

*Substitute 1 shot of espresso for coffee
— do not reduce, just add to the Nutella and orange.

BROCCOLI CHEESE SOUP

YIELDS: 2 1/2 QUARTS

Tbsp	Butter
1/4 cup	Canola Oil
1 cup	Onions, diced
2 tsp	Garlic, minced
1/2 tsp	Paprika
1/2 tsp	Kosher Salt
1/2 tsp	Black Pepper
4 Tbsp	Flour
1 cup	Potato, peeled and large diced
1	Bay Leaf
1 1/4 cups	Broccoli
2 quarts	Chicken Stock *(page 130)*
1/2 cup	Sharp Cheddar Cheese, shredded
1/4 cup	Parmesan Cheese
1 tsp	Dijon Mustard
1 1/2 Tbsp	Cornstarch, blended with 1/4 cup water
1 cup	Broccoli Florets, small pieces
1 cup	Heavy Cream

- Heat a soup pot over medium-high heat
- Add oil, butter and onions, sauté until onions begin to sweat
- Add garlic, paprika, salt and pepper, cook 2 minutes
- Sprinkle and blend flour into vegetable mixture and cook for 4 minutes
- Add potato, broccoli and bay leaf
- Add chicken stock, blend well, bring to a boil, reduce heat, simmer until the potatoes and broccoli are soft
- Puree soup with an immersion blender
- Add mustard, cheeses, cornstarch, cream and broccoli florets
- Simmer an additional 5 minutes
- Adjust seasoning to taste with salt and pepper

SAVE AND FREEZE THE BROCCOLI STEMS:

- Peel the stems to remove the tough skin and roughly chop
- Place in freezer bags, save to use for the pureed portion of the soup

THIS SOUP IS A REAL CROWD PLEASER

Chef Salad

SERVES: 1 TO 2 PEOPLE

There are many different stories of how this old-time classic originated, but this classic salad brings back childhood memories of my mom ordering this at Wanamaker's in Philadelphia. **BEEF TONGUE WAS ONE OF THE MEATS. AS A CHILD, I THOUGHT THAT WAS SCARY, BUT AT 6, MY CULINARY ADVENTUROUS SPIRIT KICKED IN AND I HAD TO TRY IT!**

1 1/2 cups	Lettuce, favorite mix
2 slices	Ham, julienne
2 slices	Turkey, julienne
1 slice	Swiss Cheese, julienne
1 slice	Cheddar Cheese, julienne
1/2	Hard-Boiled Egg, cut in wedges
2	Cherry Tomatoes, halved
2 slices	Cucumbers, circle cut
1 Tbsp	Carrot, shredded
3 Tbsp	1000 Island Dressing *(page 135)* or your favorite vinaigrette

- Place lettuce in the bottom of a salad bowl
- Arrange all the ingredients on top
- Serve with the dressing on the side

Chef Sandwich

SERVES: 1 TO 2 PEOPLE

2 slices	Bread* (rye, wheat or white)
2 Tbsp	1000 Island Dressing *(page 135)*
1 leaf	Lettuce (or shredded iceberg)
2 slices	Ham
2 slices	Turkey
2 slices	Roast Beef
1 slice	Swiss Cheese
1 slice	Cheddar Cheese
1	Hard-Boiled Egg, sliced
2 slices	Tomatoes
2 slices	Cucumber, thin bias cut
To taste	Sprinkle Salt and Pepper
1 Tbsp	Shredded Carrots

- Spread both sides bread with dressing
- Place lettuce on top of bottom slices
- Top lettuce with meats and chesses
- Top cheese with egg slices, tomatoes, salt and pepper, cucumber and shredded carrots
- Top with remaining slice of bread, cut in half

*Substitute soft roll for bread.

MOROCCAN CHICKEN VEGETABLE SOUP

YIELDS: 3 QUARTS

1/4 cup	Canola oil
1 cup	Chicken Breast - raw, diced
1/2 tsp	Black Pepper
1 tsp	Kosher Salt
1/2 cup	Onions, diced
2 tsp	Garlic, minced
1/2 cup	Carrots, diced
1/4 cup	Celery, diced
1 tsp	Ginger - ground
1 tsp	Cumin - ground
1/4 tsp	Saffron
1/2 tsp	Cinnamon - ground
1/2 tsp	Paprika
2 cans (14 oz)	Fire Roasted Tomatoes
1/4 cup	Red Pepper
1/4 cup	Green Pepper
1/2 cup	Zucchini
1 can (15 oz)	Chickpeas
1 1/2 quarts	Chicken Stock *(page 130)*
1	Lemon, zest and juice
2 Tbsp	Cornstarch, blended with 1/4 cup water

- Heat a soup pot over medium high-heat and add canola oil
- Sprinkle chicken with salt and pepper, sauté until brown on all sides
- Add onions, garlic and celery, sauté until vegetables begin to sweat
- Add carrots and dry spices, cook for 3 minutes to bloom the spices
- Add peppers, zucchini and tomatoes
- Add chickpeas and chicken stock, bring to a boil, reduce heat and simmer 15–20 minutes
- Add lemon zest, lemon juice and cornstarch, simmer for 5 minutes
- Adjust seasoning with salt and pepper to taste

TO SERVE:

- Top with a dollop of yogurt and sprinkle with feta cheese
- Serve with warm flat bread

MAKE THIS A BOWL:

- Ladle soup over couscous and top with feta or goat cheese

Orange Olive Salad

SERVES: 2 TO 3 PEOPLE

2	Oranges, peeled and sliced
1/4 cup	Red Onions, shaved
1/4 cup	Moroccan Olives
2 cups	Greens — Arugula, Spinach or Field Greens
3 Tbsp	Harissa* Vinaigrette *(page 134)*

- Mix the greens with the harissa vinaigrette
- Top with sliced oranges, shaved red onions and Moroccan olives
- Optional: Top with 2 Tbsp feta cheese

GREAT WITH GRILLED TURKEY, CHICKEN OR LAMB – MARINATE WITH GROUND CUMIN, CINNAMON, GARLIC, OLIVE OIL, SALT, PEPPER AND LEMON.

*Harissa

A SPICY AND AROMATIC CHILI PASTE THAT'S A STAPLE CONDIMENT IN NORTH AFRICAN AND MIDDLE EASTERN COOKING.

Recipes vary between countries but usually include a blend of hot chili peppers, garlic, olive oil and spices, like cumin, coriander, caraway and mint, and possibly tomato.

CURRIED PUMPKIN SOUP WITH SHIITAKE MUSHROOMS

YIELDS: 2 QUARTS

1/4 cup	Canola Oil
1/2 cup	Leeks, thin half-moon slices
1 cup	Shiitake Mushrooms, sliced
1 tsp	Garlic, minced
1 Tbsp	Curry Powder
1/2 tsp	Cinnamon - ground
1 tsp	Cumin - ground
1/2 tsp	Ginger - ground
1 tsp	Kosher Salt
1/2 tsp	Black Pepper
2 cans (14 oz)	Pumpkin
1 can (14 oz)	Coconut Milk
1 quart	Vegetable Stock *(page 131)*
2 tsp	Cornstarch, blended with 1/4 cup water
1 cup	Heavy Cream

- Heat a soup pot over medium-high heat with canola oil
- Sauté leeks and garlic until they begin to sweat
- Add shiitake mushrooms and spices, sauté for 2 minutes to bloom spices
- Add pumpkin, coconut milk and vegetable stock
- Bring to a boil, reduce heat, simmer for 15 minutes
- Add the cornstarch and cream
- Cook an additional 5 minutes
- Adjust seasoning to taste with salt and pepper
- Serve with a wedge of lime
  (For added spice, drizzle the top with Sriracha® sauce)

MAKE IT VEGAN

SUBSTITUTE ALMOND OR SOY MILK FOR HEAVY CREAM.

Maple Tofu Wrap

MAKES: 4 WRAPS

WRAP:

4	Whole Grain Tortillas
1 recipe	Maple Tofu *(recipe below)*
1 recipe	Wilted Kale *(recipe below)*
1	Apple, thinly sliced

MAPLE TOFU:

1 pkg	Tofu*
3/4 cup	Maple Mustard Marinade *(recipe below)*

- Cut firm tofu into finger-size strips
- Toss with Maple Marinade
- Let sit for 30 minutes or overnight
- Preheat oven to 375°F
- Oil/spray a baking pan, place tofu in pan
- Roast for 12 minutes
- Remove tray from oven, toss and brush with extra marinade, continue roasting 10–12 minutes or until golden brown
- Cool

WILTED KALE:

1 cup	Julienne Kale
1/4 cup	Shredded Carrots
1/8 cup	Red Onions
2–3 Tbsp	Maple Mustard Marinade
To taste	Kosher Salt & Fresh Ground Black Pepper

- Warm marinade in microwave and pour over the vegetables, toss and marinate a minimum of 20 minutes

ASSEMBLY:

- Lightly warm wrap on a griddle pan
- Spread 1 Tbsp maple mustard marinade on top of wrap
- Top with kale 3/4 way across wrap
- Arrange tofu on top of kale and top with apple slices
- Roll wrap and cut in 1/2 to serve

*Substitute tofu for pulled chicken, turkey or pork.

Maple Mustard Marinade

YIELDS: 1 1/2 CUPS

MIX TOGETHER:

1 cup	Maple Syrup
2 Tbsp	Country Dijon Mustard
1/2 tsp	Crushed Red Pepper Flakes
1/4 cup	Orange, zest and juice
1/4 cup	Olive Oil

CREAMY LEMON CHICKEN & RICE SOUP

YIELDS: 3 QUARTS

1/4 cup	Canola Oil
1/2 cup	Onion, diced
1 Tbsp	Garlic, minced
1 cup	Basmati Rice
1 cup	Mushrooms, halved, then sliced
1 sprig	Thyme - fresh
1	Bay Leaf
1 tsp	Kosher Salt
1/2 tsp	Black Pepper
2 quarts	Chicken Stock *(page 130)*
1 Tbsp	Lemon Zest
1/4 cup	Lemon Juice
1 quart	Heavy Cream
1 cup	Cooked Chicken, diced
1/2 cup	Tomatoes - fresh, small diced
1 Tbsp	Flat Leaf Parsley, chopped
2 tsp	Cornstarch, blended with 1/4 cup water

- Heat a soup pot over medium-high heat and add canola oil
- Add onions and garlic and lightly sauté
- Add rice and sauté for 1 minute
- Add mushrooms, thyme, bay leaf, salt and pepper, cook 3 minutes
- Add chicken stock, bring to a boil and simmer until the rice is tender
- Add lemon zest, lemon juice and cornstarch
- Cook for 5 minutes
- Remove half the soup and place in a container for garnish
- Puree the soup left in the pot, then add the garnish portion back into the pot
- Add heavy cream, chicken, tomatoes and parsley
- Season to taste with salt and pepper
- Simmer for 4 minutes

Basmati Rice

A LONG GRAIN RICE THAT ORIGINATED FROM INDIA.
It is available in both brown and white,
with brown being a little healthier option.

THE NUTTY FLAVOR, TEXTURE AND AROMA OF THE
BASMATI RICE ELEVATE THIS SOUP TO A GOURMET TREAT.

Roasted Eggplant Sandwich

YIELDS: 4 SANDWICHES

SANDWICH:

4	Ciabatta Rolls
2 Tbsp	Olive Oil
1 cup	Arugula
12 slices	Roasted Eggplant
12 slices	Marinated Tomatoes
4 Tbsp	Feta Cheese

EGGPLANT: *(3 slices for each sandwich)*

- Preheat oven to 400°F
- Strip eggplant leaving some skin still on, slice 1/3 inch thick
- Toss with balsamic vinaigrette, salt and pepper
- Layout on an oiled/sprayed sheet pan, roast in oven for 10 minutes, flip and roast another 8–10 minutes, until eggplant is soft but not mushy
- Cool

MARINATED TOMATOES:

- Slice 2 plum tomatoes into 6 slices each, place in a bowl
- Sprinkle with salt and black pepper
- Toss with 1 Tbsp capers, 1/4 cup chopped country olive mix and 1/4 cup of balsamic vinaigrette *(page 135)*

ASSEMBLY:

- Split ciabatta rolls
- Brush with olive oil and toast in oven or griddle pan
- Top with arugula, eggplant, tomatoes and feta cheese
- Top with bread and cut in half

Greek Dinner Salad

SERVES: 4 TO 6 PEOPLE

IN A BOWL, TOSS:

3 cups	Romaine and/or Iceberg Lettuce
1 cup	Cucumbers, striped with peeler, cut in half, seeds removed, sliced on bias 1/2 inch wide
1 cup	Tomatoes, large diced or Cherry Tomatoes cut in half
1/4 cup	Red Onion, thin julienne strips
1/2 cup	Red Wine Vinaigrette *(page 134)*
1/2 tsp	Oregano Leaves - dry
To taste	Fresh Ground Black Pepper

TOP WITH:

4 Tbsp	Feta Cheese, crumbled
8	Pepperoncini
12	Kalamata Olives

COCONUT FISH CHOWDER

YIELDS: 1 1/2 QUARTS

South American Flavors

THIS SOUP IS A FUN TWIST ON TRADITIONAL CREAMY CHOWDERS.

I'VE PAIRED THIS WITH A GRAPEFRUIT AVOCADO SALAD, BUT YOU CAN EASILY SUBSTITUTE MANGO OR PAPAYA.

1/4 cup	Canola Oil
1/2 cup	Leeks, diced
1/4 cup	Celery, small diced
1/2 cup	Sweet Potatoes, small diced
1/4 tsp	Red Pepper Flakes
2 tsp	Diced Jalapeño or Serrano Pepper
1/2 tsp	Kosher Salt
1 can (14 oz)	Coconut Milk
1 cup	Fish Stock *(page 131)* or Water
1 Tbsp	Cornstarch, blended with 1/4 cup water
1 lb	Cod or Red Snapper
1 Tbsp	Lime Zest
3 Tbsp	Lime Juice - fresh
2 Tbsp	Cilantro, chopped
1/2 cup	Tomatoes - fresh, diced

- Heat a soup pot over medium-high heat and add canola oil
- Add leeks, celery and sweet potatoes and begin to sauté
- Add the red pepper flakes, salt, and jalapeño or Serrano pepper and sauté until leeks are translucent
- Add coconut milk, stock and cornstarch
- Bring to a boil, reduce heat, simmer until the sweet potatoes are tender
- Add fish, lime zest and juice and cook for approximately 5–7 minutes or until the fish is cooked through
- Fold in the cilantro and tomatoes
- Season to taste with salt and pepper

FOR A SPICIER SOUP:

- Top soup with thinly shaved slices of jalapeño pepper and serve with a wedge of lime.

Grapefruit Avocado Salad

SERVES: 3 TO 4 PEOPLE

TOSS TOGETHER:

1	Grapefruit, peeled and segmented
1	Avocado, sliced
2 Tbsp	Red Onion, fine julienne
2 cups	Bibb Lettuce
4 Tbsp	Chipotle Vinaigrette *(page 134)*

Pão de Queijo (Brazilian Cheese Buns)

YIELDS: 14 TO 18 BUNS

THESE TAKE LITTLE TIME, ARE FUN TO MAKE, DELICIOUS AND GLUTEN FREE.

1/2 cup	Butter, unsalted
1/4 cup	Water
1/4 cup	Milk
1 tsp	Kosher Salt
2 cups	Tapioca Flour *(starch)*
2/3 cup	Aged Parmesan or Asiago Cheese, grated
2	Eggs - large

- Preheat oven to 375°F and lightly grease a sheet pan
- In a saucepan, place the butter, water, milk and salt together
- Cook over medium-high heat and bring to a boil
- Place tapioca flour in a mixing bowl with paddle attachment
- Pour boiled mixture over the tapioca flour and beat at high speed until mixture becomes elastic looking *(this happens quickly)*
- Beat in cheese, then slowly add eggs one at a time, beating until well combined and smooth
- Scoop approximately 1 oz portion on greased sheet pan, leaving space to spread
- Bake approximately 20 minutes or until golden brown
- Serve hot

They make great breakfast egg sandwiches, so make a few extra for the next day.

MOM'S CHICKEN NOODLE SOUP

YIELDS: 4 QUARTS

TAKE TIME TO MAKE A HOMEMADE CHICKEN STOCK.

It makes a huge difference in flavor and that little touch of schmaltz *(chicken fat)* just says homemade.

1/4 cup	Canola Oil
1 cup	Onions, diced
1/2 cup	Celery, straight cut
1 cup	Carrots, circle cut
1 sprig	Thyme - fresh
2	Bay Leaves
1/2 tsp	Black Pepper
1/2 tsp	Kosher Salt
3 quarts	Chicken Stock *(page 130)*
1 Tbsp	Cornstarch, blended with 1/4 cup water
2 cups	Baby Spinach
1 1/2 cups	Chicken
2 cups	Egg Noodles, cooked
2 Tbsp	Parsley, chopped

- Heat a soup pot over medium-high heat with canola oil
- At the same time, bring a pot of salted water to boil and cook egg noodles
- To the soup pot, add the onions and celery, sauté until vegetables begin to sweat
- Add the carrots, salt, pepper, and herbs, cook for 2 minutes
- Add the chicken stock, bring to a boil, reduce heat, simmer for 15-20 minutes
- Add cornstarch, cook for 3 minutes
- Add chicken, spinach and parsley, cook for another 3 minutes, then add noodles
- Season to taste with salt and pepper

Pasta* in Soup:

- To keep the integrity of the pasta, it is best to cook and chill pasta separately
- Fold cold cooked pasta into hot soup right before serving.

*Always cook pasta in salted water.

If freezing Soup:

- Portion cold pasta into the individual containers and top with cold soup.

Fun Twists to add to Classic Chicken Soup:

- Fresh basil and diced tomatoes
- Shaved slices of jalapeños, corn and lime
- Mushrooms and fennel sautéed with carrots
- Saffron and cinnamon with a squeeze of fresh orange
- Dill, lemon and red pepper
- Ginger and cilantro
- Substitute for noodles — Rice, Quinoa, Barley or Wild Rice

Matzo Balls

YIELDS: 10 TO 12 BALLS

- Replace egg noodles with Matzo Balls, in the recipe for Mom's Chicken Noodle.

When I worked at Whole Foods®, we made thousands of Matzo Balls for the Jewish Holidays. It was always a question whether you made sinkers or floaters – heavy, dense matzo balls or light, delicate and delicious.

KEYS TO SUCCESS:

- Measure everything perfectly *(follow the quantities on the package)*
- Use sparkling water and add a touch of freshly chopped dill and minced or grated onion
- Roll the balls and let chill at least 20 minutes before cooking
- Cook in a mixture of half water and half chicken stock
- Give plenty of room in the pot for the matzo balls to simmer for a good 20–25 minutes
- Cool and then place in the hot soup when serving

LOADED SWEET POTATO SOUP

YIELDS: 2 1/2 QUARTS

I LIKE THIS FUN TWIST ON A CLASSIC

Loaded Baked Potato Soup, which to me is a little heavy and rich. The balance of sweet and savory with just a touch of cream is lighter but still satisfying.

THIS SOUP WOULD PAIR WELL WITH BARBECUED PORK, CLUB SANDWICH, CLASSIC WEDGE, OR APPLE KALE SALADS.

2 1/2 cups	Baked Sweet Potatoes
1/4 cup	Canola Oil
1 1/2 cups	Bacon, raw, diced
1 cup	Onions, diced
1/2 cup	Celery, diced
2 tsp	Garlic, minced
2	Bay Leaves
2 sprigs	Thyme - fresh
1 tsp	Black Pepper
1 tsp	Kosher Salt
1 cup	Yukon Gold Potatoes, small diced
1/2 cup	Red Pepper, small diced
1 Tbsp	Pure Maple Syrup
1 Tbsp	Sherry Vinegar
1 1/2 quart	Chicken Stock *(page 130)*
1 Tbsp	Cornstarch, blended with 1/4 cup water
1 cup	Cream
1/2 cup	Green Onions, thin circle cut

- Preheat oven to 375°F
- Wash and bake sweet potatoes on a tray until very soft, let cool, remove skin and set aside
- Heat a soup pot over medium-high heat and add canola oil and bacon
- Cook bacon, stirring occasionally for even cooking, remove from the pan and set aside to add back later
- Add onions to the bacon drippings and sauté
- Add celery and garlic, sauté until vegetables begin to sweat
- Add herbs and spices, cook for 1 minute
- Add potatoes, red pepper, maple syrup and sherry vinegar, cook for 2 minutes
- Add the baked sweet potatoes
- Slowly add the chicken stock and blend together
- Bring to a boil, reduce heat, simmer for a good 15-20 minutes, until potatoes are soft
- Add cornstarch, cream, cooked bacon and green onions, simmer for about 5 minutes
- Season to taste with salt and pepper

SERVING IDEA:

- Top with green onions, bacon and shredded white cheddar cheese.

BBQ Pork Sliders

YIELDS: 12 SANDWICHES

1 lb	Pulled Pork, purchase or smoke/cook your own
5 oz	Barbecue Sauce, favorite
12	Hawaiian Rolls
1/2 cup	Pickled Red Onions *(recipe below)*

- Split buns and fill with pulled pork that is lightly tossed in barbecue sauce
- Topped with pickled red onions
- Serve extra sauce on the side

OPTIONAL TOPPINGS:

- Sliced dill pickles, cole slaw, cheddar or smoked gouda cheese

Pickled Red Onions:

1 cup	Onion, julienne
1/2 cup	Apple Cider Vinegar
2 Tbsp	Sugar
1 tsp	Kosher Salt
1/4 tsp	Crushed Red Pepper

- Mix vinegar, sugar, salt and red pepper
- Pour over onions and toss
- Marinate at least 4 hours - best overnight or store up 10 days in refrigerator

Adobo Black Bean with Corn Salsa

YIELDS: 2 1/2 QUARTS

2 Tbsp	Canola Oil
1 cup	Onions, diced
2 tsp	Garlic, chopped
2 tsp	Cumin - ground
1/2 tsp	Paprika
1 Tbsp	Chipotle in Adobo, pureed
1 lb	Black Beans* - dry, rinsed
3 quarts	Vegetable Stock *(page 131)*
1/2 cup	Poblano Peppers, diced
1/2 cup	Red Peppers, diced
1/4 cup	Cilantro, chopped
2 Tbsp	Lime Juice
2 Tbsp	Honey *(for vegan, substitute Agave Nectar)*
1/2 tsp	Black Pepper
1 tsp	Kosher Salt

- Heat soup pot over medium-high heat
- Add canola oil and toast the cumin and paprika for 30 seconds
- Add onions and garlic, sauté until onions begin to sweat
- Add chipotle in adobo and black beans
- Add stock and bring to a boil, reduce heat, simmer until beans become tender
- Once beans are tender, remove 1 cup of beans for garnish and puree the rest
- Add the garnish beans, peppers, cilantro, honey, lime juice, salt and pepper *(if soup is too thick, add more stock)*
- Simmer for 10–12 minutes
- Adjust seasoning to taste with salt and pepper
- Top each bowl with a Tbsp of Corn Salsa

*Soaking beans overnight will reduce cooking time and ease digestion.

Jicama Orange Salad

Jicama Orange Salad

SERVES: 4 TO 6 PEOPLE

IN A BOWL, LAYER:

2 cups	Jicama, julienne
1/4 cup	Red Pepper, small diced
1/4 cup	Green Onion, thin circle cut
1 Tbsp	Cilantro, roughly chopped or tear leaves into to small pieces

WHISK TOGETHER:

1 oz	Orange Juice
1 oz	Lime Juice
1 tsp	Salt
1/2 tsp	Chili Powder
1 oz	Olive Oil

- Toss with jicama and refrigerate for a minimum of 30 minutes

PLATING:

4	Naval Oranges, peeled and circle cut

- Place orange slices on a platter and top with jicama
- **Optional:** Place oranges on a bed of greens, spinach or kale lightly tossed in the dressing and following plating above

Cheesy Quesadillas

SERVES: 2 TO 3 PEOPLE

- Mix 1 cup Mexican cheese with 1 Tbsp cilantro
- Place 1/2 cup cheese in the center of two 8-inch round flour tortillas and spread evenly to the edge
- Top with another tortilla and lightly press
- Heat a griddle/frying pan over medium-high heat and brush with oil
- Place the tortilla in center of pan and brown on one side, turn and brown on the other for 1 1/2 to 2 minutes per side
- Cut into wedges
- **FOR A FUN TWIST:** Add sliced or diced fresh tomatoes, fresh or canned green chilies or grilled julienne bell pepper

Corn Salsa

YIELDS: 2 3/4 CUPS

1 cup	Corn *(best grilled and cut off the cob)*
1 cup	Tomatoes, diced
1/4 cup	Onion, diced
1 Tbsp	Jalapeño, minced *(double for extra heat)*
1/2 cup	Salsa Verde
2 Tbsp	Cilantro
1/2	Lime

- In a bowl, toss all ingredients together
- Adjust seasoning with salt, pepper and lime juice to taste

BEEF MUSHROOM BARLEY

YIELDS: 3 1/2 QUARTS

A LOAF OF CRUSTY BREAD STUDDED WITH ROASTED GARLIC IS MY FAVORITE FOR DIPPING INTO THIS HEARTY SOUP.

1/4 cup	Canola oil
8 oz	Beef* *(Chuck or Top Sirloin)*, large diced
1/2 tsp	Black Pepper
1/2 tsp	Kosher Salt
1/2 cup	Onions, diced
2 tsp	Garlic, minced
1 1/2 cups	White Mushrooms
1 cup	Portobello Mushrooms, gills scraped with a spoon and small diced
1/2 cup	Carrots, circle cut
1/4 cup	Celery, straight cut
1 can (14 oz)	Petite Tomatoes, diced
2 sprig	Thyme - fresh
2	Bay Leaves
2/3 cup	Barley
1 cup	Red Wine *(optional)*
4 quarts	Beef Stock *(page 130)*
2 Tbsp	Parsley, rough chopped

- Heat a soup pot over medium-high heat with canola oil
- Add the beef, sprinkle with salt and pepper, brown on all sides
- Add onions, garlic and mushrooms, sauté until vegetables begin to sweat
- Add celery, carrots and herbs, cook for 3 minutes to bloom spices
- Add red wine, cook for 2 minutes
- Add barley, tomatoes, then beef stock
- Bring to a boil, reduce heat, simmer until the barley is tender
- Add parsley and adjust seasoning with salt and pepper to taste

*Substituting a variety of wild mushrooms in place of the white mushrooms will add texture and flavor.

MAKE IT VEGAN

OMIT BEEF AND SUBSTITUTE MUSHROOM OR VEGETABLE STOCK FOR THE BEEF STOCK. ADD A VARIETY OF WILD MUSHROOMS *(about 2 cups)* IN PLACE OF THE BEEF.

Ranch House Salad

SERVES: 2 TO 3 PEOPLE

2 cups	Romaine Lettuce
1/4 cup	Cucumbers, diced
2 Tbsp	Carrots, shredded
1/4 cup	Tomatoes, diced
1/2 Tbsp	Red Onion, shaved
1/4 cup	Corn *(best grilled and cut off the cob)*
2 Tbsp	Shredded Cheddar Cheese
1/2 cup	Croutons
1/4 cup	BBQ Ranch Dressing *(recipe below)*

- Toss the romaine, cucumbers, carrots, onions, tomatoes, corn and croutons with dressing
- Sprinkle cheddar cheese on top
- **Optional:** Arrange everything on top of the lettuce with dressing on the side; Add grilled chicken or steak

BBQ Ranch Dressing

YIELDS: 1 1/2 CUPS

THIS DRESSING MAKES A GREAT SPREAD FOR A SANDWICH, WRAP OR CHICKEN SALAD.

BLEND TOGETHER:

1 cup	Ranch Dressing
1/2 cup	Smoky BBQ Sauce

LOW GLYCEMIC INDEX AND HIGH FIBER.
ITS CHEWY TEXTURE AND NUTTY FLAVOR
can be substituted easily for pasta
TO ADD MORE WHOLE GRAINS TO YOUR DIET.

NEW ENGLAND CLAM CHOWDER

YIELDS: 1 1/2 QUARTS

1 cup	Clam Meat, chopped *(purchase canned or follow recipe below)*
1/2 cup	Bacon, diced *(substitute Turkey Bacon)*
2 Tbsp	Butter
1 cup	Onions, small diced
1 tsp	Garlic, minced
1/2 cup	Celery, small diced
1/4 cup	Green Peppers, small diced
4 Tbsp	Flour
2	Bay Leaves
1 sprig	Thyme - fresh
1/2 tsp	Black Pepper
1 quart	Clam Juice*
1 1/2 cups	Red Skin Potatoes, diced
1 cup	Cream
1/2 tsp	Tabasco
1 Tbsp	Parsley - fresh, chopped
To taste	Kosher Salt and Pepper

- In a soup pot over medium-high heat, cook the bacon, remove to add back later
- Add butter to the bacon drippings, then onions, sauté until onions start to sweat
- Add celery, garlic and green pepper, sauté 2 minutes
- Add thyme and bay leaves, sauté 2 minutes
- Sprinkle and blend flour into vegetables, reduce heat, cook for 4 minutes
- Slowly add the clam juice, blend well with the vegetable mixture to avoid flour lumps
- Add clams and potatoes, bring to a boil, reduce heat, simmer 10-12 minutes or until potatoes are soft
- Add cream, cooked bacon, Tabasco and parsley and cook for 4-5 minutes
- Adjust seasoning to taste with salt and pepper

*If cooking whole clams, save the cooking liquid, add water or clam juice if needed.

How to cook clams:

- Scrub approximately 14-16 clams, place in a soup pot and cover with 1 1/2 cups water
- Cook for about 3-5 minutes, clams will open
- Transfer clams to a bowl to cool, save the juice for soup but run through a fine mesh strainer
- Remove clams from the shell and roughly chop
- Discard any unopened clams

Entertaining Ideas:

Serve soup in warn bread boules. The bread gets smothered with the creamy soup and a hint of garlic oil *(page 137)* **— DELICIOUS!**

Boules:

- Hollow out the insides of small sourdough boules
- Brush insides with garlic butter
- Bake until boules are crunchy inside, 10–15 minutes

Pair with:

- Salad - A platter of Iceberg Wedges or Spinach Salad
- Dessert - Keep the New England theme and serve Monster Cookies *(page 41)*

Classic Wedge Salad

SERVES: 1 PER PERSON

ASSEMBLE:

- Place wedge on a plate
- Spoon 2–3 Tbsp dressing on top

TOP WITH:

1 Tbsp	Diced Tomatoes
1 Tbsp	Julienne Bacon
1 Tbsp	Blue Cheese
1 tsp	Green Onion

DRESSING OPTIONS:

- Red wine vinaigrette, dijon vinaigrette or creamy blue cheese dressing

PREP THE WEDGE:

- Remove any large outside leaves
- Core the head of iceberg lettuce
- Rinse in cold water, place in a bowl with the core facing down so it can drain
- Cover and refrigerate for a good hour to let the lettuce crisp
- Cut lettuce head in half, then cut each half into 3 to 4 wedges

OTHER WEDGE IDEAS:

- 1000 Island Dressing *(page 135)* with hard-boiled eggs, shredded carrot and tomato
- Avocado Ranch Dressing *(page 135)* with grilled corn, tomato and black bean

SPRING GREENS SOUP

YIELDS: 3 QUARTS

MY SISTER'S FAVORITE!

Add white beans or quinoa to give this garden delight a boost of protein.

Not a vegetarian?

- Add a smoked turkey leg or wing with the greens and simmer in soup.

1/4 cup	Canola Oil
1/2 cup	Onions, diced
1/4 cup	Celery, diced
1 Tbsp	Garlic, minced
1 can (14 oz)	Petite Diced Tomatoes
1 bag (5 oz)	Baby Spinach
1 bunch	Escarole, 1- to 1 1/2-inch pieces
2 bunch	Chard, Collard or Dandelion Greens, 1-inch pieces
1 bunch	Kale, julienne
2 1/2 quarts	Vegetable Stock *(page 131)*
2	Lemons, zest and juice
1 sprig	Thyme - fresh
1/4 cup	Basil, chopped
1/4 cup	Balsamic Vinegar
1 Tbsp	Sugar
1/2 tsp	Salt
1/2 tsp	Crushed Red Pepper Flakes
2 Tbsp	Cornstarch, blended with 1/4 cup water

- Heat a soup pot over medium-high heat with canola oil
- Add onions and garlic, sauté until onions begin to sweat
- Add greens and sauté
- Add salt, pepper, herbs and tomatoes
- Add balsamic vinegar and sugar, cook for 4 minutes
- Add stock, bring to a boil, reduce heat and simmer for 15 minutes
- Add cornstarch, spinach, lemon zest and juice
- Simmer another 3 minutes
- Adjust seasoning to taste with salt and pepper

Greens* have a lot of grit & sand and need to be washed thoroughly!

- Rinse the greens first to remove initial grit
- Fill a bowl with cold water
- Remove the tough stems and place greens in bowl of cold water
- Gently stir with a spoon or hand to loosen the grit
- Let sit a few minutes so all the grit sinks to the bottom, then lift the greens off the top
- Tear or cut to desired size

*Leeks are processed similar to greens.

BBQ Chicken Club

SERVES: 1 TO 2 PEOPLE

THE SMOKY FLAVOR FROM THE BACON AND BBQ MAYO PAIRS GREAT WITH ALL THE GREENS IN THE SPRING GREENS SOUP.

2 slices	Sourdough or Multigrain Bread
1	Grilled Chicken Breast, bias cut (4-5 oz)
3 slices	Tomato
1 leaf	Lettuce
2 slices	Bacon *(cooked crisp)*
2 Tbsp	BBQ Mayo *(recipe below)*
To taste	Salt and Pepper

- Toast the bread and spread with BBQ Mayo on both sides
- Top the bottom slices with grilled chicken, leaf lettuce, tomato, salt, pepper and bacon strips
- Top with remaining slice of bread and cut in half
- **Optional:** Add avocado or sliced cheddar or pepper jack cheese

Simple BBQ Mayo

YIELDS: 2 CUPS

THIS IS A GREAT DRESSING FOR A CHICKEN SALAD.

BLEND TOGETHER:

1 cup	Mayonnaise
1 cup	Barbecue Sauce *(your favorite)*

TACO SOUP

YIELDS: 3 1/2 QUARTS

While writing this book, a friend told me about a Taco Soup that was served at Boy Scotts of America® meetings for years.

I admit I was a little hesitant but found it to be really tasty, quick and easy, and it feeds a large crowd. **BOB, I HOPE YOU LIKE MY VERSION!**

1/4 cup	Canola Oil
1 cup	Onions, diced
1 Tbsp	Garlic, minced
3 tsp	Chili Powder
1 1/2 tsp	Cumin - ground
1 tsp	Paprika
1 tsp	Black Pepper
1/2 tsp	Kosher Salt
1 lb	Ground Beef
3 Tbsp	Flour
1 1/2 quarts	Beef Stock* *(page 130)*
2 cups	Salsa *(your favorite)*
1 can (14 oz)	Diced Tomatoes with Green Chilies
1 can (15 oz)	Kidney Beans, drained and rinsed
1 can (15 oz)	Pinto Beans, drained and rinsed
4 tsp	Cornstarch, blended with 1/4 cup water
2 cups	Cheddar and Jack Cheese, shredded
1/4 cup	Cilantro, chopped

- Heat soup pot over medium-high heat with canola oil
- Add onions, sauté until onions begin to sweat
- Add spices and garlic, sauté for 2 minutes to bloom
- Add ground meat and brown - don't overstir, beef should be pea-size crumbles
- Sprinkle flour and blend, cook for 2 minutes
- Slowly add beef stock and blend
- Add tomatoes and beans
- Bring to boil, reduce heat and simmer for about 15-20 minutes
- Add cornstarch, cheese and cilantro
- Simmer for 4 minutes
- Season to taste with salt and pepper
- Ladle in a bowl and add your choice of toppings

*Add Beer - Use 2 cups Beer and 1 quart of Beef Stock.

Taco Soup Options:

- For a meatier version, increase beef to 2 lb
- Try a combination of beef and pork
- Substitute ground turkey or chicken and use Chicken Stock *(page 130)* for Beef Stock

Taco Soup Topping Ideas:

- Tortillas, lightly broken or cut into strips
- Avocado, sliced or diced
- Shredded Cheese
- Sour Cream
- Shredded Iceberg Lettuce or Napa Cabbage
- Shaved thin slices of Fresh Jalapeño
- Fresh Cilantro
- Fresh Tomatoes, diced
- Onions, diced
- Green Onions, circle cut
- Corn Salsa *(page 75)*
- Fritos
- Cheese Quesadilla

Zesty Mexican Chocolate Rice Pudding

YIELDS: 1 QUART

I was taught this method for making rice pudding from a coworker at Whole Foods®. She said her abuela taught her when she was a young girl. Slowly simmering the rice with milk and spices on the stove really melds all the flavors, creating a rich and creamy treat. Once cold, if it is a little thick, add milk to reach desired consistency.

I KICKED UP HER RECIPE WITH CHOCOLATE AND A HINT OF CHIPOTLE POWDER.

 **Substitute soy or your favorite nut milk to make it vegan.**

1 cup	Rice
6 cup	Milk
3/4 cup	Sugar
3 Tbsp	Cocoa Powder
1/2 tsp	Cinnamon - ground
1/4 tsp	Chipotle Powder *(optional)*
2 strips	Orange Peel, 1/2-inch wide strips *(remove the bitter white pith)*
2	Cinnamon Sticks
1/4 tsp	Kosher Salt
1 1/2 tsp	Pure Vanilla Extract

- Place rice, milk, sugar, cocoa powder, cinnamon, chipotle powder, lemon peel, cinnamon sticks and salt in a heavy-gauge sauce pan and stir well
- Over medium heat bring to a low boil, stir well, reduce heat and simmer until rice is tender and milk has been absorbed *(Stir often for even cooking and to prevent sticking to the button or sides of the pan)*
- Remove from heat, stir in vanilla and cool
- If needed, add additional milk to reach your desired consistency

PULLED CHINESE CHICKEN VEGETABLE SOUP

YIELDS: 3 QUARTS

KICK UP THE HEAT!

Drizzle sriracha sauce on top of each bowl along with a cilantro sprig and lime.

Make it a bowl:

Ladle the soup over cooked jasmine rice or Asian noodles.

1/4 cup	Canola Oil
2 1/2 tsp	Toasted Sesame Oil
1 cup	Onions, sliced 1/4 inch wide by 1 inch long
1/2 cup	Celery, bias slice
1/4 cup	Ginger - fresh, minced or grated
2 cups	Bok Choy, bias sliced including leaves
1 1/2 Tbsp	Chili Garlic Sauce
3/4 cup	Carrots, julienne or shredded
1/2 cup	Red Peppers, sliced 1/4 inch wide by 1 inch long
1/2 cup	Water Chestnuts, sliced
1 can (7 oz)	Bamboo Shoots
2 quarts	Chicken Stock *(page 130)*
1/2 cup	Soy Sauce
2 Tbsp	Cornstarch, blended with 1/4 cup water
2 Tbsp	Cilantro, chopped
1 cup	Edamame*

OPTIONAL:

2 cups	Leftover Rotisserie Chicken, pulled, or Cooked Chicken Breast, bias sliced

- Heat a soup pot over medium high-heat with canola oil
- Add onions, ginger, celery and sesame oil, sauté until onions begin to sweat
- Add chili garlic sauce and bok choy
- Add carrots, red peppers and chicken stock
- Bring to a boil, reduce heat, and simmer for 10 minutes
- Add soy sauce, cornstarch, water chestnuts, and bamboo shoots
- Cook 3 minutes, then add cilantro, edamame and optional chicken
- Season to taste with salt and pepper
- Simmer an additional 2 minutes

*Edamame will yellow sitting overnight or freezing. To keep the color, add when reheating.

Pulled Chinese Chicken Vegetable Soup

Cheaters Scallion Pancakes

YIELDS: 4 PANCAKES *(16–24 WEDGES)*

A SIMPLE AND EASY TWIST ON A TRADITIONAL DISH.

8	Tortillas (6-inch)
3/4 cup	Green Onions, thin circle cut
1 Tbsp	Cilantro, chopped
1 tsp	Sriracha Sauce
1/2 tsp	Sesame Oil
1	Egg Yolk
As needed	Water
As needed	Oil, for griddling

- In a bowl, combine and blend sesame oil, egg yolk and sriracha sauce
- Add the cilantro and green onions
- Lay out 4 tortillas and brush with water
- Divide mixture among the 4 tortillas, spread evenly
- Top each with remaining tortilla, lightly press down, and chill for 10 minutes
- Over medium heat, lightly oil/spray the griddle pan
- Cook pancakes until golden brown, flip and brown the other side, approximately 3 minutes per side
- Cut each pancake into wedges
- Serve with Dipping Sauce *(recipe below)*

Dipping Sauce

YIELDS: 1/2 CUP

WHISK TOGETHER:

1/4 cup	Soy Sauce
1/4 cup	Rice Wine Vinegar
2 tsp	Ginger - fresh, grated
1 tsp	Honey
1 tsp	Sesame Oil
1/2 tsp	Orange Zest

LEEK & POTATO

YIELDS: 1 1/2 QUARTS

SERVE THIS SOUP HOT OR COLD.
If cold, top with a dollop of sour cream and sprinkle with fresh chives.

Any variety of potato will work for this soup. I prefer Yukon Gold for the rich buttery flavor, and using baby redskin potatoes for the diced garnish will add contrast in color and texture.

4 Tbsp	Butter
2 cups	Leeks, split and small diced
1 tsp	Garlic, minced
2 cups	Potatoes, peeled and cubed
3 Tbsp	Flour
1	Bay Leaf
1 sprig	Thyme - fresh
1/2 tsp	Kosher Salt
1/2 tsp	Black Pepper
1 quart	Chicken Stock *(page 130)*

GARNISH:

1 cup	Potatoes, small diced
1/2 cup	Leeks, small diced
1/2 cup	Carrots, small diced
1 Tbsp	Parsley
1 cup	Heavy Cream
1/2 tsp	Kosher Salt
1/2 tsp	Black Pepper

- Heat a soup pot over medium-high heat
- Add butter, leeks and garlic, sauté until the leeks begin to sweat
- Add thyme, bay leaf, salt and pepper, cook for 2 minutes
- Sprinkle flour and blend with vegetables
- Cook for 3 minutes, stirring to prevent vegetables from sticking to the bottom and burning
- Add stock and mix well
- Add potatoes, bring to a boil, reduce heat and simmer until the potatoes are soft
- Puree with immersion blender until smooth — the starch level in potatoes will vary, so if mixture is too thick, add stock to desired consistency
- Add the garnish vegetables and cook for approximately 8 minutes, until vegetables are soft
- Add heavy cream and parsley
- Adjust seasoning to taste with salt and pepper

NOTE: If freezing, add 1 Tbsp cornstarch blended with 1/4 cup water when adding the cream and simmer for 3 minutes. This helps stop cream from separating when reheating.

BLT Salad Crostini

YIELDS: 10 TO 12 CROSTINI

CROSTINI:

1 loaf	French Bread, long bias cut
1–2	Garlic Cloves, smashed
As needed	Olive Oil
To taste	Kosher Salt and Black Pepper

- Cut bread, rub both sides with garlic and brush with olive oil
- Sprinkle with salt and pepper
- Let sit until you prepare the salad

SALAD:

Toss together:

1 1/2 cups	Field Greens *(substitute Arugula)*
2 cups	Tomatoes, diced, or Cherry Tomatoes cut in half *(multicolor looks best)*
8 strips	Bacon, cooked and julienne 1/2-inch wide pieces
1/4 cup	Balsamic Vinaigrette *(page 135)*

ASSEMBLY:

- Griddle the bread on both sides until golden brown and crunchy
- Place on a platter
- Pile the salad mixture on top of the bread
- **Optional:** Sprinkle top with your choice of blue, goat, Parmesan or sharp cheddar cheese

HARIRA

YIELDS: 2 QUARTS

1/4 cup	Canola Oil
1 lb	Lamb, cubed 1/2 inch
1/2 cup	Onions, diced
1/4 cup	Celery, diced
1/2 cup	Carrots, diced
1 tsp	Kosher Salt
1/2 tsp	Black Pepper
1	Bay Leaf
1 tsp	Ginger - fresh, grated
1 tsp	Turmeric
1/2 tsp	Cinnamon - ground
1/2 tsp	Cumin - ground
1/2 tsp	Smoked Paprika
2 Tbsp	Tomato Paste
1 can (14 oz)	Fire Roasted Tomatoes
1 1/2 quarts	Chicken Stock *(page 130)*
1/2 cup	Lentils
1 can (15 oz)	Chickpeas
1/2 cup	Vermicelli Pasta* (thin Spaghetti), broken into 1 1/2-inch pieces
1 Tbsp	Cilantro, chopped
1 Tbsp	Parsley - fresh chopped
2 Tbsp	Lemon Juice
1 tsp	Lemon Zest
2	Eggs, beaten

- Heat soup pot over medium-high heat and add canola oil
- Add lamb, sprinkle with salt and pepper, and brown on all sides
- Add onions, garlic and celery, sauté until vegetables begin to sweat
- Add carrots and spices, sauté for 3 minutes to bloom spices, until carrots begin to sweat
- Add tomato paste and cook 2 minutes
- Add tomatoes, lentils and chicken stock
- Bring to a boil, reduce heat, simmer 10 minutes
- Add chickpeas and pasta, cook for 10 minutes — pasta should be al dente
- Add cilantro, parsley and lemon
- Season to taste with salt and pepper
- Whisk the beaten eggs into the soup
- Cook an additional 2 minutes

*If freezing, cook pasta separately. Fold into cold soup.

Suggested Servings:

- Pair this soup with a simple green salad tossed in Harissa Vinaigrette *(page 134)*, fresh dates, figs, almonds and/or warm flatbread.
- I've added a simple orange date salad that you can use for a salad or dessert.

Harira

A TRADITIONAL MOROCCAN SOUP
THAT IS EATEN TO "BREAK FAST" DURING RAMADAN.

Harira is a very filling soup with lentils, chickpeas, meat, tomatoes, pasta and traditional Moroccan spices.

I've made this soup with lamb, but you can easily substitute beef or chicken.

Moroccan Orange Date Salad

SERVES: 4 PEOPLE

4	Oranges
8	Dates, stoned and sliced
1/3 cup	Marcona Almonds
1	Lemon - fresh juice
1 tsp	Sugar
1/4 tsp	Cinnamon - ground

- Peel oranges and cut into circles, remove seeds
- In a bowl mix lemon juice, sugar and cinnamon. Toss with dates and oranges
- Let marinate for about 15 minutes
- Toss with almonds and serve

SERVING IDEAS:

- Nest ingredients on a bed of field greens, Bibb lettuce or baby spinach
- Add a dollop of Greek yogurt on the side

ROASTED TOMATO BASIL SOUP

YIELDS: 2 1/2 QUARTS

1 1/2 quarts	Tomatoes, large pieces
3 cloves	Garlic, smashed
1 cup	Red Onion, large pieces
2 Tbsp	Olive Oil
1 tsp	Kosher Salt
1/2 tsp	Black Pepper
1 can (6 oz)	Tomato Paste
2 Tbsp	Balsamic Vinegar
2 quarts	Vegetable Stock *(page 131)*
10	Basil Leaves
2 Tbsp	Honey*
2 Tbsp	Cornstarch, blended with 1/4 cup water
1 tsp	Kosher Salt
1 tsp	Black Pepper

- Heat oven to 375°F
- Spray a roasting pan with cooking spray for easy cleanup
- Place tomatoes, onions and garlic in pan and toss with the oil, salt and pepper
- Roast in oven for 30 minutes
- Remove from the oven, add tomato paste and balsamic vinegar
- Stir and return to oven for 20–30 minutes, until tomatoes are caramelized but not charred
- Remove from oven, place all ingredients in a soup pot, then rinse the roasting pan out with vegetable stock and add to soup pot
- Add vegetable stock, honey and basil
- Bring to a boil, reduce heat, simmer for 20–25 minutes
- Add cornstarch, salt and pepper, simmer 3–5 minutes
- Depending on the sweetness of the tomatoes, add more honey if necessary
- Adjust seasoning with salt and pepper to taste

* Substitute Agave Nectar to make soup vegan.

Cobb Sandwich

SERVES: 1 TO 2 PEOPLE

2	Challah, Brioche Roll or sliced bread
3–4 slices	Turkey
1–2 leaf	Bibb Lettuce
2–3 slices	Tomato
1/4	Avocado, thin slices
1	Hard-Boiled Egg, sliced
2 strips	Bacon
2 Tbsp	Blue Cheese Mayo
To taste	Salt and Pepper

- Split each roll and spread the Blue Cheese Mayo on inside of each slice
- Top one slice with lettuce, turkey, tomatoes, egg, salt, pepper, avocado and bacon
- Top with other slice and cut in half

Blue Cheese Mayo

BLEND TOGETHER:

1/2 cup	Mayonnaise
2 Tbsp	Blue Cheese, crumbled
Pinch	Black Pepper

Savory Asparagus Goat Cheese Tart

SERVES: 6 TO 8 PEOPLE

GREAT FOR ENTERTAINING!

It looks fancy but is really simple, easy and delicious.

1 sheet	Puffed Pastry
1/2 cup	Caramelized Onions *(recipe below)*
2 oz	Goat Cheese
1/4 cup	Swiss Cheese, shredded
1/2 cut	Asparagus, cut into 1 1/2- to 2-inch pieces
8	Pear Tomatoes, cut in half
1/2 cup	Parmesan Cheese, shredded
1	Egg, blended with 2 Tbsp water

- Preheat oven to 385°F
- Lightly fold caramelized onions, Swiss cheese and goat cheese together
- Thaw puffed pastry for about 15-20 minutes
- Lay out on a parchment-lined sheet pan
- Lightly press or roll with a rolling pin to even out the dough
- With a fork, dock* the puffed pastry, leaving a 1/2-inch border around the outside
- Brush pastry dough with egg-water mixture
- Spread the onion and cheese mixture on the bottom inside the border
- Scatter the asparagus and tomato on top
- Sprinkle with Parmesan cheese
- Bake about 25-30 minutes, until it puffs and becomes a nice golden brown
- Let slightly cool before cutting
- **Optional:** Make individual tarts by cutting dough into 6 or 9 pieces leaving only 1/4 inch rim around outside of each piece

*Dock by poking holes around the dough to stop dough layers from rising when baked.

Caramelized Onions

2 cups	Onions, julienne
2 Tbsp	Olive Oil
1 tsp	Fresh Thyme, chopped
1/2 tsp	Salt
1/4 tsp	Black Pepper

- Heat olive oil in a sauté pan
- Add onions, sauté until they just start to sweat
- Add thyme, salt and pepper and slowly cook until onions become soft and slightly brown
- Remove from heat and cool

SPINACH, BACON & MUSHROOM SOUP

YIELDS: 3 QUARTS

1 Tbsp	Canola Oil
1 1/2 cups	Bacon, julienne
1/2 cup	Onions, diced
2 tsp	Garlic, minced
3 cups	Mushrooms, sliced
1/2 tsp	Black Pepper
1/2 tsp	Kosher Salt
1 sprig	Thyme - fresh
2	Bay Leaves
1/4 cup	Flour
2 quarts	Chicken Stock *(page 130)*
1/2 cup	Red Pepper
8 oz	Spinach
2 Tbsp	Cornstarch, blended with 1/4 cup water
2 cups	Heavy Cream

- Heat a soup pot over medium-high heat and add canola oil
- Add the bacon and cook until bacon is fully cooked, remove bacon to add back later
- Add onions, garlic and mushrooms, sauté until the vegetables begin to sweat
- Add the herbs and spices, cook for 2 minutes
- Sprinkle and blend flour to create a roux
- Cook for 4 minutes
- Slowly add 2-3 cups chicken stock, blend well to prevent lumps, then add remaining stock
- Bring to a boil, reduce heat, simmer 10 minutes
- Add spinach, red pepper and cooked bacon
- Add cornstarch and heavy cream, cook for 5 minutes
- Season to taste with salt and pepper

I created this recipe for my uncle many years ago after drawing his name for the family Christmas gift exchange. Living near Kennet Square, Pennsylvania (known as the mushroom capital of the world), mushroom soup was a favorite.

THE ADDITION OF BACON & SPINACH TAKES CLASSIC MUSHROOM SOUP TO A WHOLE NEW LEVEL. ADD EVEN MORE DEPTH TO THE SOUP BY USING A VARIETY OF DOMESTIC & WILD MUSHROOMS.

Butternut Arugula Salad

SERVES: 3 TO 4 PEOPLE

A GREAT SALAD TO SERVE WITH GRILLED OR ROASTED TURKEY, PORK OR CHICKEN.

2 cups	Roasted Butternut Squash *(recipe below)*
2 cups	Arugula
1	Green Apple, thinly sliced
1/4 cup	Toasted Almonds or Walnuts
4 Tbsp	Sherry Vinaigrette *(page 135)*

- Toss arugula, squash and apples with dressing
- Top with toasted nuts
- **Optional:** Sprinkle goat or blue cheese on top

This salad makes a tasty wrap or sandwich:

- Warm multigrain tortilla*
- Top with salad, roll and cut in half
- **Optional:** Add blue, goat or Swiss cheese; Add roasted or grilled turkey, pork or chicken

*Substitute toasted ciabatta or multigrain roll for tortilla.

Roasted Butternut Squash

YIELDS: 2 CUPS

2 cups	Butternut Squash, peeled and diced
1/2 cup	Onion, diced
2 Tbsp	Sage - fresh, chopped
1/2 tsp	Kosher Salt
1/4 tsp	Black Pepper
2 Tbsp	Olive Oil

- Preheat oven to 400°F
- Toss all ingredients together
- Spread in a single layer on a sheet pan
- Roast for 7 minutes, stir, continue roasting for another 4-5 minutes, until squash is soft but still firm
- Cool

SIMPLE GAZPACHO SOUP

YIELDS: 1 1/2 QUARTS

TRADITIONALLY, GAZPACHO IS THICKENED WITH BREAD.

This recipe is bread-free with no added carbs or gluten.

1	European Cucumber, seeds removed
1/2	Green Pepper, large
1/2	Red Pepper, large
2 cups	Tomatoes, fresh, cored
1/2	Jalapeños, seeds removed *(leave in seeds for spicier soup)*
1/2 cup	Onion
1 clove	Garlic
2 cups	Tomato or Vegetable Juice
1/2 cup	Cilantro
1 Tbsp	Sherry Vinegar
1	Lime, zest and juice
2 Tbsp	Olive Oil
To taste	Kosher Salt
To taste	Black Pepper

- Take 1/3 of cucumber, peppers and tomatoes, dice into 1/4-inch pieces and set aside for garnish
- Large dice the rest of the vegetables, puree in a food processor or blender, then pour into a large bowl
- Add the tomato or vegetable juice, garnish vegetables, cilantro, sherry vinegar, lime, salt, pepper and olive oil and blend together
- Adjust seasonings to taste with salt and pepper
- Chill for a minimum of 45 minutes before serving

Egg, Avocado + Tomato Sandwich

Egg, Avocado & Tomato Sandwich

SERVES: 1 TO 2 PEOPLE

A PERUVIAN FRIEND TAUGHT ME HOW TO MAKE THIS SANDWICH.
THE SIMPLE FLAVORS BLEND PERFECTLY FOR A DELICIOUS LIGHT SUMMER MEAL.

2 slices	Bread, white or wheat
1 leaf	Bibb Lettuce
1	Hard-Boiled Egg, sliced
3 slices	Tomato
1/4	Avocado, sliced
2 Tbsp	Cilantro Mayo *(recipe below)*
To taste	Kosher Salt
To taste	Black Pepper

- Spread one slice of bread with cilantro mayo
- Top with lettuce, tomato, egg and avocado
- Sprinkle with salt and pepper
- Top with the remaining slice of bread and cut in half
- **Optional:** Add bacon or grilled shrimp

 Save some calories and make the sandwiches open-faced.

Cilantro Mayo

BLEND TOGETHER:

1 cup	Mayonnaise
1/4 cup	Cilantro, chopped
1	Lime, zest and juice

Peach Cobbler (Biscuit Style)

SERVES: 6 TO 8 PEOPLE

PEACHES:

5 cups	Peaches, peeled and sliced
3/4 cup	Sugar, granulated
2 tsp	Candied Ginger, minced
1	Lime, zest and juice

BISCUIT DOUGH:

1 1/2 cups	Flour
1 Tbsp	Sugar, granulated
1 Tbsp	Baking Powder
1/2 tsp	Salt
4 Tbsp	Butter
1	Egg
1/4 cup	Milk

TOPPING:

3 Tbsp	Sugar, granulated

- Preheat oven to 400°F
- Spray or butter a baking dish
- Add peaches, sugar, ginger and lime to dish and lightly mix
- Bake for about 15 minutes
- Mix biscuit topping in a bowl, blending dry ingredients, then cut butter into flour mixture until it resembles a coarse meal
- Mix egg and milk, gently fold into flour mixture
- Remove baked peaches from oven, spoon biscuit dough on top, sprinkle with sugar
- Return to oven and bake for another 20-25 minutes, until top is golden brown and firm
- Serve warm with whipped cream or ice cream

NEW YEAR'S BLACK-EYED PEA SOUP

YIELDS: 2 1/2 QUARTS

A Southern Tradition!

Eating black-eyed peas on New Year's Day is said to bring you good luck throughout the year.

PAIR WITH A PAN OF WARM CORNBREAD AND HONEY BUTTER *(page 27)*.

THIS RECIPE IS A TWIST OFF THE CLASSIC.

With the addition of greens and added stock, this soup has a healthier halo. If you don't eat pork, substitute turkey bacon or add a smoked turkey leg to simmer with the black-eyed peas.

1 cup	Smoked Ham, diced *(substitute Bacon)*
1/4 cup	Canola Oil
1 cup	Onions, diced
1 cup	Carrots, diced
1/2 cup	Celery, diced
1 tsp	Garlic, minced
2	Bay Leaves
1 sprig	Thyme - fresh
1/2 tsp	Black Pepper
1/2 tsp	Paprika
1 can (14 oz)	Tomatoes, diced
2 1/2 quarts	Chicken Stock *(page 130)*
2 cups	Black-Eyed Peas, cooked
1 bag (5 oz)	Baby Greens
1 Tbsp	Cornstarch, blended with 1/4 cup water

- Heat a soup pot over medium-high heat with canola oil
- Add the ham, sauté to lightly brown
- Add the onions, carrots, celery and garlic until the vegetables begin to sweat
- Add the spices and sauté for 2 minutes
- Add tomatoes, black-eyed peas and chicken stock
- Bring to a boil, reduce heat, simmer 15–20 minutes
- Add cornstarch and greens
- Simmer 4 minutes
- Adjust seasoning to taste with salt and pepper

THE CLASSIC VERSION:

You can make a more traditional version by following the Senate Bean Soup recipe *(page 26)* and substituting the black-eyed peas for the white beans.

Maple Baked Apples

YIELDS: 6 SERVINGS

3	Apples*
1	Orange, juiced
1/2 tsp	Cinnamon - ground
6 Tbsp	Maple Syrup
1/2 cup	Nutty Granola *(recipe below)*

Maple Baked Apples

- Preheat oven to 350°F
- Core apples, trim a small amount off the top and bottom to sit flat, then cut in half
- Spray/butter a baking pan and arrange apples in pan
- Squeeze the orange juice over the apples
- Sprinkle apples with cinnamon and drizzle 1 Tbsp maple syrup over each apple half
- Cover in foil and bake for 15 minutes
- Remove tray from oven, remove foil, turn the apples over, spoon syrup in the bottom of the pan back over the apples
- Return to oven, without foil, and bake 15–20 minutes *(apples should be soft but not mushy)*
- Top each apple with Nutty Granola and cook 5 minutes
- **Optional:** serve with ice cream, mascarpone or yogurt

*Substitute peaches, plums or figs for apples. These fruits will take less time to bake than an apple.

Nutty Granola

YIELDS: 1 QUART

1 1/2 cups	Rolled Oats
1/2 cup	Raw Whole Almonds, rough chopped
1/2 cup	Raw Walnuts, rough chopped
1/2 cup	Raw Pecans, rough chopped
3/4 cup	Coconut *(unsweetened is best)*
1/2 cup	Pure Maple Syrup
1 Tbsp	Olive Oil
1/2 tsp	Kosher Salt
1/2 tsp	Cinnamon - ground

- Preheat oven to 325°F
- In a large bowl, whisk maple syrup, olive oil, salt and cinnamon
- Add the nuts*, coconut and oats, toss until everything is coated
- Spread out a thin layer on sheet pan, bake for 30–40 minutes, stirring every 10 minutes, until granola is evenly browned
- Cool and store in a sealed container

**Substitute nuts, seeds or spice, fold in your favorite dried fruit for added taste and texture.*

MUSHROOM, LEEK & APPLE BISQUE

YIELDS: 2 QUARTS

 This two-step soup is worth washing the additional soup pot.

FOR TRUE INDULGENCE:

When serving, top soup with brie cheese and diced crisp apple.

3 Tbsp	Canola Oil
2 Tbsp	Butter
1 lb	Button Mushrooms, sliced *(save 1 cup for garnish)*
1 lb	Cremini *(Baby Bella)* Mushrooms, sliced
1 1/2 cups	Leeks, diced *(save 1/2 cup for garnish)*
4 Tbsp	Flour
1	Bay Leaf
1/2 sprig	Thyme - fresh
1 cup	White Wine, dry not sweet
1 quart	Mushroom Stock or substitute Vegetable Stock *(page 131)*
1/2 tsp	Salt
1/2 tsp	Black Pepper
1 cup	Apple, small diced
1 tsp	Dijon Mustard
1 cup	Heavy Cream
1 Tbsp	Cornstarch, blended with 1/4 cup water

BASE:

- Heat a soup pot over medium-high heat
- Add 2 Tbsp canola oil and butter
- Add leeks and sauté until leeks begin to sweat
- Add mushrooms, thyme and bay leaf, sauté until the mushrooms begin to soften
- Sprinkle and blend flour into the mushroom mixture, reduce heat and cook 4 minutes, stirring so bottom does not burn
- Slowly add wine, blend with the mushroom mixture, then add the stock
- Bring to a boil, reduce heat, simmer for 15–20 minutes
- Puree soup

FINAL:

- Heat a soup pot over medium-high heat with 1 Tbsp canola oil
- Add 1/2 cup leeks, sauté until they begin to sweat
- Add 1 cup sliced mushrooms, sauté until they begin to sweat
- Add apple and 1/2 cup white wine, simmer for 4 minutes
- Add soup base, bring to a boil, then reduce heat to simmer
- Add Dijon mustard, cornstarch and cream, simmer for 3 minutes
- Adjust seasoning to taste with salt and pepper

Crusty Ham Baguette

SERVES: 2 TO 4 PEOPLE

1	Baguette
4 slices	Ham* *(French or Black Forest Ham)*
3 Tbsp	Dijon Butter *(depends on bread size)*

- Split the baguette in half and spread both sides with the Dijon butter
- Arrange a single layer of ham on top of one side
- **Optional:**
  Add cheese — Gruyere, Swiss or Brie
  Add vegetable — Spinach, Blanched Asparagus or Broccolini
- Top with bread and cut

*Substitute smoked turkey or prosciutto for ham.

Dijon Butter

1 Stick	Butter (1/2 cup)
1 Tbsp	Dijon Mustard

- Soften butter, fold in the mustard

A CLASSIC FRENCH SANDWICH!

The key to this sandwich is a loaf of fresh, crusty bread. Look for ficelles {skinny baguettes} or pull out some of the center of the bread to keep the meat-to-bread ratio balanced.

THREE ONION SOUP

YIELDS: 2 1/2 QUARTS

2 Tbsp	Canola Oil
1 stick	Butter (1/2 cup)
1 quarts	Sweet Onions, julienne
3 cups	Red Onions, julienne
1 cup	Leeks, thin half-moon slices
2 tsp	Garlic
1/2 tsp	Black Pepper
1/2 tsp	Kosher Salt
2	Bay Leaves
1 sprig	Thyme - fresh
7 Tbsp	Flour
1/4 cup	Balsamic Vinegar or 1/2 cup White Wine
2 quarts	Beef Stock *(page 130)*
1 quarts	Chicken Stock *(page 130)*

- Heat a soup pot over medium-high heat
- Add the canola oil, butter and onions, sauté until onions begin to sweat
- Add garlic, black pepper, thyme, bay leaf and salt, cook 2 minutes
- Reduce heat and slowly cook onions until they wilt and begin to caramelize to a nice golden brown *(at least 15 minutes)*, stirring often so onions do not burn
- Sprinkle and blend flour into onion mixture to create a roux, cook for 5 minutes
- Add balsamic vinegar or white wine, slowly blend into the onion mixture, then add 1 quart of the stock, blend thoroughly to eliminate any flour lumps
- Add the rest of the stock, bring to a boil, reduce heat and simmer for 15–20 minutes
- Adjust seasoning with salt and pepper to taste
- **Optional:** Finish with 1/2 to 1 cup heavy cream

This soup is easy to make Vegan!

- Substitute Mushroom and Vegetable Stock for Beef and Chicken stock *(page 131)*
- Substitute oil for butter

Pretzel Cheese Croutons

- Preheat oven to 375°F
- Slice pretzel bread* 1/2 inch thick and place on baking tray
- Blend 1/4 cup canola oil with 1 Tbsp mustard and brush bread on both sides
- Top with shredded sharp white cheddar or Swiss cheese
- Bake for 10–12 minutes

*Substitute a baguette for pretzel bread.

Apple Kale Salad

SERVES: 2 TO 3 PEOPLE

FOR A DELICIOUS TREAT, MAKE THIS SALAD WITH HONEYCRISP APPLES WHEN THE FRESH FALL CROP IS JUST ARRIVING IN THE MARKET.

The secret to this salad:

- Use a firm sweet/tart apple
- Very thin slices of apple, suggest using a mandolin or Microplane®
  (store slices in ice cold water to stay crisp and prevent browning)

1 1/2 cup	Kale, julienne
4 Tbsp	Champagne or Honey Mustard Vinaigrette *(page 134)*
1 cup	Apple*, shaved
1 oz	Aged Sharp Cheddar Cheese

- Toss the kale with the dressing, let sit about 20 minutes to soften
- Taste and add salt and pepper, then toss with the apple slices
- Top with shaved slices of aged sharp cheddar cheese
- **Optional:** Add in toasted nuts, shaved red onion, dried cranberries, golden raisins or currants

*Substitute pears for the apples and blue cheese for the cheddar.

CHILLED AVOCADO SOUP

YIELDS: 1 1/4 QUARTS

PERFECT SUMMER SOUP

Serve with a pitcher of margaritas or sangria.

Serving Suggestions:

- Garnish with a fanned cherry tomato and fresh cilantro leaves
- Top with corn tomato salsa
- Top with grilled shrimp, lime wedge and fresh cilantro leaves
- Serve with a platter of cheese quesadillas or basket of tortilla chips

2 cups	Avocado
3/4 cup	Roasted Poblano Pepper
1 (5.6 oz)	Plain Greek Yogurt
2 cups	Vegetable Stock *(page 131)*
1	Lime, zest and juice
1/2 tsp	Kosher Salt
1/4 tsp	Black Pepper
1 Tbsp	Cilantro - fresh, chopped
1/2 cup	Tomato - fresh, small diced

- Place the avocado, roasted pepper and yogurt in a blender
- Blend until smooth
- Slowly add the vegetable stock to reach the desired consistency
- Pour into a bowl, fold in salt, lime zest and juice, cilantro and tomatoes
- Adjust seasoning with salt and pepper to taste
- Chill for a minimum of 30 minutes

Black Bean & Corn Salad

SERVES: 3 TO 4 PEOPLE

1 can (15 oz)	Black Beans, drained and rinsed
1 cup	Corn *(best off the cob)*
1 Tbsp	Green Onions, thin circle cut
1/2 cup	Cherry Tomatoes, halved
1/2 cup	Jicama, small diced
1 cup	Cabbage, shredded or Slaw Mix
1 Tbsp	Cilantro, chopped
2	Limes, zest and juice
1 oz	Extra Virgin Olive Oil
1 tsp	Kosher Salt
1/4 tsp	Smoked Paprika

- In a large bowl, layer all the vegetables
- In a small bowl, whisk the olive oil, lime zest and juice, salt and paprika
- Pour over the vegetables and toss
- **Optional:** Sprinkle with queso blanco; Spoon into Bibb lettuce cups, and sprinkle with queso blanco

Pineapple Coconut Bread Pudding with White Chocolate Drizzle

YIELDS: 2 QUART PAN *(SERVES 6 TO 8 PEOPLE)*

1 1/2 quarts	Day-Old Bread, cubed
2 cans (8 oz)	Crushed Pineapple, packed in juice not syrup
1 cup	Coconut, shredded
1/2 cup	Almonds, toasted
1 stick	Butter (1/2 cup), unsalted and melted
3/4 cup	Brown Sugar
4	Eggs, beaten
1/4 cup	White Chocolate, melted

- Preheat oven to 350°F
- Spray or butter a baking dish
- In a bowl, mix the bread, pineapple with juice, almonds and coconut
- In a separate bowl, whisk eggs, brown sugar and melted butter
- Pour over bread mixture, toss and place in baking dish
- Bake for about 40-45 minutes until top is golden brown and firm
- Drizzle top with melted white chocolate
- Best served hot from the oven

ESCAROLE SAUSAGE & TORTELLINI SOUP

YIELDS: 4 QUARTS

THIS SOUP PAIRS PERFECTLY WITH A CLASSIC CAESAR SALAD, CRUSTY BREAD AND A GLASS OF RED WINE.

1/4 cup	Canola Oil
1 lb	Italian Sausage, sweet or hot as desired
1 cup	Onion, diced
1/4 cup	Celery, diced
2 tsp	Garlic, minced
1/2 tsp	Black Pepper
1/2 tsp	Dry Oregano
1/2 tsp	Kosher Salt
1/4 tsp	Crushed Red Pepper Flakes
2	Bay Leaves
1 sprig	Rosemary - fresh
1 sprig	Thyme - fresh
1 cup	Zucchini, diced
1 cup	Carrots, diced
1 1/2 quarts	Escarole, 1-inch pieces
2 quarts	Chicken Stock *(page 130)*
1 can (14 oz)	Tomatoes, diced
1/2 quart	Water
1 cup	Tortellini* - dry
3 Tbsp	Basil - fresh, chopped
1	Lemon, zest from all
2 Tbsp	Lemon Juice

- Cook sausage links on the stove or in the oven, let cool and slice into 1/2-inch circles
- Heat a soup pot over medium-high heat with canola oil
- Add onions and celery, sauté until they start to sweat
- Add garlic, herbs and spices, sauté for 2 minutes
- Add zucchini, carrots and escarole, sauté until they start to sweat
- Add tomatoes, chicken stock and water
- Bring to a boil, add tortellini and sausage, reduce heat, simmer 12–15 minutes
- Add basil, lemon zest and juice
- Adjust seasoning to taste with salt and pepper
- Serve soup with freshly grated Parmesan cheese

***SUBSTITUTE FRESH TORTELLINI:**

- Omit the water from the recipe
- Add sausage, simmer for 8 minutes, then add tortellini and cook for 5 minutes
- Finish with basil and lemon zest and juice

Bruschetta

YIELDS: 3 CUPS

2 cups	Tomatoes, diced
1 cup	Cherry Tomatoes, circle cut
2 cloves	Garlic, thinly shaved
1/4 cup	Extra Virgin Olive Oil
1/2 cup	Basil - fresh
1	Lemon, zest and juice
To taste	Kosher Salt
To taste	Black Pepper

- Place the garlic and canola oil in a sauté pan, slowly heat on a low burner until the garlic is soft but not brown
- Remove from the heat and place in a bowl
- Top with the tomatoes, lemon, basil, salt and pepper, lightly toss
- Adjust seasoning to taste with salt and pepper
- Serve with Grillled Crostini Bread *(page 137)* or Parmesan Cheese Bread *(page 17)*

The key to great bruschetta is TASTY TOMATOES!

- **Use a COLORFUL VARIETY, VARY CUTS and SIZES of tomatoes**
- **If tomatoes are bland, ADJUST THE AMOUNT OF LEMON, SALT & PEPPER or add a SPLASH OF BALSAMIC VINEGAR to POP THE FLAVOR**
- **MAKES A GREAT SALAD by eliminating the bread and tossing with ARUGULA or another FAVORITE GREEN**

CHICKEN POT PIE SOUP

YIELDS: 2 1/2 QUARTS

COMFORT FOOD AT ITS BEST!

Serve with a simple Garden Salad & Blackberry Peach Cobbler to give the meal that final Southern touch.

1 cup	Chicken: raw, boneless skin off, diced
1 tsp	Salt
1 tsp	Black Pepper
1 cup	Onion, diced
1 tsp	Garlic, diced
1 cup	Celery, straight cut
1 cup	Carrots, circle cut
1/4 cup	Canola Oil
4 Tbsp	Butter (1/2 stick)
1	Bay Leaf
1 sprig	Thyme - fresh
5 Tbsp	Flour
1 1/4 quarts	Chicken Stock *(page 130)*
1 1/2 cups	Potatoes, peeled and diced
2 tsp	Sage - fresh, fine julienne
2 Tbsp	Cornstarch, blended with 1/4 cup water
1/4 cup	Heavy Cream
1 Tbsp	Parsley, chopped
1 cup	Green Peas, frozen

- Heat a soup pot over medium-high heat
- Add canola oil, butter and chicken
- Sprinkle chicken with salt and pepper and lightly brown
- Add onions, sauté until they begin to sweat
- Add celery, garlic, bay leaf and thyme, cook for 2 minutes
- Sprinkle flour and blend in
- Reduce heat, cook for 3 minutes, stirring frequently to prevent burning
- Slowly add a portion of stock, blending well to prevent flour lumps, then add rest of stock
- Add carrots, potatoes and sage, bring to a boil, reduce heat, simmer until the potatoes are tender
- Add cornstarch, cream and parsley, cook for 4 minutes
- Adjust seasoning to taste with salt and pepper
- Fold in green peas and serve

TO SERVE:

- Ladle soup into a bowl
- Break the pie crust into 1 1/2- to 2-inch pieces and place on top of soup
- **Optional:** Top pie crust with cheddar cheese or your favorite herb before baking

Pie Crust for Chicken Pot Pie Soup:

TOPS 6 TO 8 BOWLS

1 sheet	Pie Dough
1	Egg
1 Tbsp	Water
1/4 tsp	Kosher Salt
1/8 tsp	Black Pepper
1/8 tsp	Paprika

- Preheat oven to 375°F
- Place the pie dough on a sheet pan
- Whisk egg and water, then brush dough with egg wash
- Sprinkle with salt, pepper and paprika
- Bake until golden brown, approximately 18-20 minutes
- Cool for at least 5 minutes before breaking

Blackberry Peach Cobbler {cake style}

SERVES: 6 TO 8 PEOPLE

FRUIT FILLING:

1 1/2 cups	Peaches - fresh or frozen, sliced
1 cup	Blackberries - fresh or frozen
1 Tbsp	Sugar
1 tsp	Cinnamon - ground

BATTER:

4 Tbsp	Butter (1/2 stick)
3/4 cup	Flour
3/4 cup	Sugar
1 tsp	Baking Powder
1/4 tsp	Salt
3/4 cup	Milk
1/4 tsp	Vanilla Extract

- Preheat oven to 350°F
- Toss fruit with cinnamon and sugar, set aside
- Place baking dish in the oven to melt the butter, swirl around to coat
- In a bowl, mix dry ingredients
- Add the milk and vanilla extract, whisk together
- Pour into buttered pan, top with fruit
- Bake for 30-40 minutes or until golden brown
- Sprinkle with powdered sugar or serve with ice cream

QUICK PHO

YIELDS: 1 1/2 QUARTS *(4 TO 6 SERVINGS)*

I MADE THIS SOUP WITH A CONTAINER OF BEEF STOCK.
HOWEVER, IF YOU HAVE TIME, MAKE THE GINGER BEEF BROTH RECIPE ON PAGE 130.

BROTH:

1 Tbsp	Canola Oil
1/2 each	Onion, cut into 4 pieces
1 piece	Ginger Root, 1-inch, cut into 4–5 slices
2 cloves	Garlic, smashed
2	Star Anise
1/4 bunch	Cilantro Stems
1/2 bunch	Basil Stems
1 piece	Lemon Grass, 1 to 2 inches
1 Tbsp	Chili Garlic Sauce
2 quarts	Beef Stock *(page 130)*
1 Tbsp	Honey
1 Tbsp	Soy Sauce

- Heat a soup pot over medium-high heat with canola oil
- Add onions, ginger, garlic and lemon grass
- Once it begins to sweat, add chili garlic sauce, herbs, stems and spices, cook for 3 minutes to bloom spices
- Add stock and bring to a boil
- Add honey and soy sauce, reduce heat and simmer over low heat for 15 minutes — stock should reduce by 1/4
- Strain

BEEF:

1 lb	Top Sirloin or Flank Steak

- For easier slicing, place steak in the freezer for 15–20 minutes to firm, but do not freeze
- Slice super thin on a bias — 45-degree angle slicing across the grain of the beef
- Keep cold until ready to serve

RICE STICK NOODLES:

8 oz	Rice Stick noodles

- Cook in boiling water, chill and set aside covered or leave soaking in cold water until needed

VEGETABLES*:

This is nontraditional, but i like the healthy addition.

1/2 cup	Zucchini, thin bias half-moon sliced
1/4 cup	Red Pepper, 1-inch thin strips
1	Baby Bok Choy, quartered
1/2 cup	Baby Carrots, thin bias sliced
1/2 cup	Shiitake Mushroom, thin sliced
1 cup	Napa Cabbage, shredded (1 inch long)

*Omit for a more traditional Pho.

TO SERVE QUICK PHO:

- Divide the cooked rice stick noodles into the soup bowls
- Heat the Pho broth, add the vegetables to the broth, cook until al dente, remove from broth and place on top of noodles in the soup bowls
- Place the raw steak on top of vegetables in each bowl
- Heat broth to boiling and ladle on top of the steak

SERVE WITH AN ARRAY OF TOPPING!

TOPPING SUGGESTIONS:

Bean Sprouts, Daikon Radishes, Micro Greens, Green Onions, Cilantro, Thai Basil, Sriracha, Lime Wedges, Shaved Jalapeños

MAKE IT VEGETARIAN

SUBSTITUTE A COMBINATION OF MUSHROOM AND VEGETABLE STOCK IN PLACE OF THE BEEF STOCK. INSTEAD OF STEAK, ADD TOFU THAT IS MARINATED AND GRIDDLED WITH GINGER, LIME AND SOY SAUCE.

DON'T FORGET THE CHOPSTICKS!

SEAFOOD BISQUE

YIELDS: 1 3/4 QUARTS

FILL A BOWL WITH ROUND CRUSTY OYSTER CRACKERS TO SERVE WITH THIS SOUP.

TO CUT THE RICHNESS, SERVE WITH A SIMPLE SALAD WITH A TART VINAIGRETTE.

1 1/2 lb	Fish and Shellfish*
4 Tbsp	Butter
1 Tbsp	Canola Oil
1 cup	Leeks, diced
1/4 cup	Celery, small diced
1 cup	Mushrooms, sliced
2 1/2 tsp	Old Bay Seasoning
1	Bay Leaf
4 Tbsp	Flour
1 cup	White Wine, dry not sweet
2 cups	Fish Stock *(page 131)* or substitute Chicken Stock *(page 130)*
2 Tbsp	Cornstarch, blended with 1/4 cup water
1/2 cup	Red Peppers, diced
2 cups	Heavy Cream
1/4 cup	Fresh Dill, chopped

- Heat pan over medium heat
- Add canola oil, butter, then add leeks, celery, mushrooms, Old Bay and bay leaf, sauté until vegetables sweat
- Sprinkle flour and blend with vegetable mixture, cook 4 minutes, stirring often so bottom does not burn
- Add white wine and stock slowly to blend into the vegetable mixture and prevent lumps
- Add half the cream and bring to a boil, reduce heat, simmer for 5-6 minutes
- Add fish, red pepper and cornstarch
- Simmer for 5-7 minutes or until fish is cooked
- Add the rest of the cream and dill
- Season to taste with salt and pepper

*Use a combination of seafood like cod or other white fish, shrimp, scallops, salmon, crab, lobster or whatever looks good at the market.
If using cooked shellfish, fold in at the end.

Watercress

As a child, I used to pick fresh watercress with my aunt in the summertime.

This super green lacks popularity in the U.S., but it is part of the same family and has the same health benefits as kale, broccoli and Brussels sprouts.

WITH ITS TENDER LEAVES, PEPPERY, SLIGHTLY BITTER FLAVOR, IT MAKES A GREAT SALAD OR SANDWICH GREEN.

Watercress can be substituted in recipes using arugula.

Watercress Soup

AN OLD-WORLD CLASSIC SOUP THAT SADLY HAS NEVER REALLY FOUND A FOLLOWING IN THE STATES, BUT GIVE IT A TRY.

TO MAKE:

- Follow the Asparagus Soup recipe on page 114 and just substitute watercress for asparagus.

Watercress Salad with Tomato Vinaigrette

SERVES: 2 TO 3 PEOPLE

1 bunch	Watercress
4 Tbsp	Tomato Vinaigrette *(page 134)*
1	Hard-Boiled Eggs, finely diced
1/4 cup	Carrots, grated

- Wash the watercress and trim stems
- Place in a bowl, top with carrots and egg, keep chilled until ready to toss
- Lightly toss with dressing
- **Optional:** Add crumbled goat or shaved pecorino cheese

GRILLED VEGETABLE BARLEY

YIELDS: 2 1/4 QUARTS

BARBECUING OVER THE WEEKEND?

Grill some extra vegetables. The smoky flavor really adds depth to this vegetarian soup. Any vegetable you grill works great in this soup. Feel free to experiment to find your favorite combination.

DON'T HAVE A GRILL? SEAR THE VEGETABLES ON A GRIDDLE PAN ON THE STOVE.

SIMPLE GRILLED VEGETABLES:
I like to toss them in equal parts canola oil and balsamic vinegar with a touch of garlic and a pinch of salt and pepper. Optional: Add some fresh chopped rosemary, thyme and/or sage. Zucchini and yellow squash, red or sweet onions, and multiple colors of bell peppers are a must, but I usually add at least two of the following: eggplant, Portobello mushrooms, carrots, corn, butternut squash, broccoli, Brussels sprouts or asparagus.

2 Tbsp	Olive Oil
1 quart	Grilled Vegetables, 1/2-inch pieces
2 tsp	Garlic, minced
2	Bay Leaves
1 sprig	Rosemary - fresh
1 sprig	Thyme - fresh
1/4 tsp	Kosher Salt
1 quart	Tomato or Vegetable Juice
1 quart	Water
1/2 cup	Barley
1 Tbsp	Honey*
1 Tbsp	Balsamic Vinegar
1/4 tsp	Crushed Red Pepper Flakes
1/4 cup	Basil - fresh, chopped
1/4 cup	Parsley - fresh, chopped
To taste	Salt and Pepper

- Heat a soup pot over medium-high heat
- Add olive oil and garlic and lightly sauté
- Add 1 cup of the grilled vegetables, herbs and spices, sauté for 2 minutes
- Add the tomato or vegetable juice, water and barley
- Bring to a boil, reduce heat, simmer for 8–10 minutes, until barley is tender but firm
- Add the rest of the grilled vegetables, honey, balsamic vinegar, and red pepper flakes, simmer another 6–8 minutes
- Adjust seasoning to taste with salt and pepper
- Add basil and parsley, simmer for 2 minutes

*Substitute Agave Nectar to make soup vegan.

Flank Steak & Arugula Sandwiches

SERVES: 2 TO 4 PEOPLE

1	Crusty Baguette
2 Tbsp	Garlic Butter
8 oz	Marinated and Cooked Flank Steak, thinly sliced on a bias *(45° angle)*
1 1/2 cups	Arugula
3 Tbsp	Wide Shaved Parmesan or Pecorino Cheese
2 Tbsp	Olive Oil
1/2	Lemon - fresh, juiced

- Preheat oven to 400°F
- Split baguette in half, brush inside with garlic butter and place on a baking pan
- Toast bread for 5-6 minutes
- Arrange the thin slices of steak end to end on one half of baguette
- In a bowl, toss the arugula with the olive oil, lemon juice and cheese
- Top steak with the arugula salad
- Add other half of baguette and cut into 2-4 sandwiches
- **Optional:** Add roasted tomatoes or Caramelized Onions *(page 91)*

Flank Steak Marinade

PERFECT FOR ONE FLANK STEAK

2 tsp	Garlic, minced
1 Tbsp	Shallots for Sweet Onion, minced
3 Tbsp	Balsamic Vinegar
1 Tbsp	Honey
1 Tbsp	Water
2 tsp	Lemon Juice
1 1/2 tsp	Rosemary - fresh, minced
1/2 tsp	Kosher Salt
1/4 tsp	Black Pepper

- Toss together In a Ziploc® bag
- Add Flank Steak and cover with marinade
- Marinate overnight or at least 4 hours
- Bring steak to room temperature before grilling to desired doneness

ASPARAGUS SOUP

YIELDS: 2 QUARTS

2 Tbsp	Butter
1 Tbsp	Canola Oil
1/2 cup	Onion, diced
1 tsp	Garlic, minced
1 quarts	Asparagus, cut into 1-inch pieces
4 Tbsp	Flour
1	Bay Leaf
1/2 tsp	Kosher Salt
1/4 tsp	Black Pepper
1 quart	Chicken Stock *(page 130)*
1 1/2 cups	Heavy Cream
1 Tbsp	Cornstarch, blended with 1/4 cup water
1/2	Lemon - fresh, zest and juice

GARNISH:

1/2 cup	Asparagus, tips and thin circle slices
3 Tbsp	Red or Yellow Bell Pepper *(optional)*, finely diced

- Heat a soup pot over medium heat
- Add canola oil, butter, onions and garlic, sauté until onions begin to sweat
- Add asparagus, salt, pepper and bay leaf, sauté until the asparagus begins to sweat
- Sprinkle flour and blend with vegetable mixture, reduce heat and cook for 4 minutes, stirring to prevent bottom from burning
- Blend in chicken stock, bring to a boil, reduce heat, and simmer for 12–15 minutes
- Puree mixture with an immersion blender
- Add cream, cornstarch and garnish asparagus and bell peppers, then simmer for 4 minutes
- Add lemon zest and juice
- Adjust seasoning to taste with salt and pepper

FOR A 5-STAR FEAST,
top the Asparagus Soup with lump crabmeat & serve with Cheese Straws *(page 33)*

Shrimp & Feta Salad

SERVES: 4 PEOPLE

SHRIMP:

1 lb	Raw Shrimp *(21–25 count)*, peeled and deveined
2 Tbsp	Garlic Oil *(page 137)*
1	Lemon, zest and juice

SALAD:

1 cup	Cherry Tomatoes, halved, or quartered if large
1 cup	Cucumbers, peeled, seeded, diced
1/4 cup	Red Onions, fine julienne
1/2 cup	Feta Cheese, crumbled *(reserve 2 Tbsp for topping)*

DRESSING:

1/2 cup	Yogurt, plain
1 Tbsp	Mint, chopped
1 Tbsp	Dill, chopped
1/4 tsp	Kosher Salt
1/4 tsp	Black Pepper

- Sauté shrimp in garlic oil for 4–5 minutes or until shrimp turn pink and opaque
- Immediately add the lemon zest and juice, remove from pan to cool
- In a large bowl, blend the dressing ingredients
- Fold the cooked shrimp into the dressing
- Let chill for at least 30 minutes
- When ready to serve, toss shrimp salad with salad vegetables, sprinkle reserved 2 Tbsp of feta cheese on top
- **Optional:** Nest in lettuce cups or stuff in pita or soft brioche rolls

EGG DROP & STRACCIATELLA SOUPS ARE VERY SIMILAR EVEN THOUGH ONE IS ASIAN & THE OTHER ITALIAN.

They both are made by bringing a rich chicken broth to a boil and slowly whisking in eggs right before serving. Both of these soups are quick and easy for A FUN DINNER ANY NIGHT OF THE WEEK.

The key is the stock!

If you have time, make the recipe for Double Chicken Stock *(page 130)*, but a box stock will work for that dinner in a hurry. ADD A COUPLE OF KEY INGREDIENTS TO INTENSIFY THE INTERNATIONAL FLAVOR PROFILES OF THESE SOUPS.

EGG DROP

* Slice and sauté a 1-inch piece of ginger and half a bunch of cilantro stems before adding the Chicken Stock

STRACCIATELLA

* Sauté 2 tsp garlic, a 2-inch piece of Parmesan rind and half a bunch of basil stems before adding the Chicken Stock

EGG DROP SOUP

YIELDS: 1 QUART

1 Tbsp	Sesame Oil
1 Tbsp	Canola Oil
2 tsp	Garlic, minced
1 1/2 Tbsp	Soy Sauce
1 quart	Chicken Stock *(page 130)*
1/2 cup	Carrots, shaved, circle cut or shredded
2 Tbsp	Cornstarch, blended with 1/4 cup water
2	Eggs, beaten
2 tsp	Sriracha Sauce
1/4 cup	Green Onions, circle cut
1/2 cup	Pulled Chicken
1 Tbsp	Cilantro, roughly chopped

- In a soup pot, slowly cook the garlic in canola and sesame oil — do not burn
- Add carrots and cook 1 minute
- Add soy sauce and chicken stock, bring to a boil, reduce heat and simmer 2 minutes
- Add cornstarch, simmer 3 minutes
- Whisk the eggs with sriracha sauce
- Rapidly whisk the soup and slowly pour the egg mixture into the soup, let sit for 30 seconds to give the eggs time to cook, then slightly stir
- Add the green onions, chicken and cilantro, simmer 2 minutes and serve
- **For added zing:** Drizzle each bowl with sriracha sauce and a squeeze of lime

ITALIAN STRACCIATELLA SOUP

YIELDS: 1 QUART

1 quart	Chicken Stock, Parmesan infused
2	Eggs, beaten
2 Tbsp	Olive Oil
1 clove	Garlic, thinly shaved
1/4 tsp	Crushed Red Pepper Flakes
2 Tbsp	Cornstarch, blended with 1/4 cup water
1/2 cup	Tomatoes - fresh, small dice
1/4 cup	Basil - fresh, chopped
2 Tbsp	Parmesan Cheese
1/2 cup	Chicken Breast, cooked, thin bias sliced
1	Lemon, zest and juice

- In a soup pot, slowly cook the garlic in the olive oil and crushed red pepper flakes
- Add the chicken stock and bring to a boil
- Add the cornstarch and simmer for 3 minutes
- Rapidly whisk broth, then slowly pour in the beaten eggs, let sit about 30 seconds before stirring to give the eggs a chance to cook
- Fold in the tomatoes, basil, Parmesan cheese, chicken and lemon
- Simmer 2 minutes and serve
- **Optional:** Sprinkle the top of the soup with additional Parmesan cheese

Keep the INTERNATIONAL FLAVORS flowing to round out the meal.

Egg Drop Soup

- Pair this soup with crispy wontons, Cheaters Scallion Pancakes *(page 85)* or Cashew Pineapple Salad *(page 43)*.

Italian Stracciatella Soup

- Pairs perfectly with a Caesar salad and Parmesan Cheese Bread *(page 17)* or Bruschetta *(page 105)*.

HOLIDAY SOUP
"ITALIAN WEDDING SOUP"

YIELDS: 4 QUARTS

Every year as a child, during the Christmas season I would help Mrs. Falini roll the little meatballs to make this delicious soup.

WE ONLY ATE THIS SOUP AT THE HOLIDAYS AND IT WAS TRULY A SPECIAL TREAT.

Rolling meatballs takes some time, but it is definitely worth it!

1/4 cup	Canola Oil
1 1/2 cups	Onions, diced
1 cup	Celery, diced
1 Tbsp	Garlic, minced
1 tsp	Red Pepper Flakes
1 tsp	Oregano, dry leaf
2	Bay Leaves
1 can (14 oz)	Tomatoes, diced
2 1/2 quarts	Chicken Stock *(page 130)*
40-50 each	Mini-Meatballs
2 cans (15 oz)	Cannellini Beans, drained and rinsed
2 Tbsp	Cornstarch, blended with 1/4 cup water
1/2 cup	Parmesan Cheese
3 cups	Baby Greens — Spinach, Kale and Escarole
1/4 cup	Basil - fresh, chopped
1/4 cup	Parsley, chopped
1/4 cup	Olive Oil

- Heat a soup pot over medium-high heat with canola oil
- Add onions and celery, sauté until vegetables begin to sweat
- Add garlic, carrots and spices, cook until garlic starts to sweat
- Add tomatoes and chicken broth
- Bring to a boil, reduce heat, simmer for 15 minutes
- Add cornstarch and Parmesan cheese, simmer 3 minutes
- Add mini-meatballs and cook until they float, approximately 4 minutes
- Add beans, greens, basil and parsley
- Cook until greens wilt but are still bright green, about 2 minutes
- Finish with olive oil and season to taste with salt and pepper
- Serve soup with freshly grated Parmesan cheese

Mini-Meatballs for Italian Wedding Soup

YIELDS: 40 TO 50 MEATBALLS

1/2 cup	Bread Crumbs
1/2 cup	Parmesan Cheese
3 Tbsp	Milk
2 Tbsp	Parsley, chopped
1 tsp	Dry Oregano
1 tsp	Kosher Salt
1 tsp	Black Pepper
2	Eggs, beaten
8 oz	Ground Beef*
8 oz	Mild Italian Sausage

- In a bowl, mix the bread crumbs, Parmesan cheese, milk and spices together
- Add beaten eggs
- Add beef and sausage, mix thoroughly
- Roll into small walnut-size balls, place on a sheet pan and chill — meatballs need to be cold before adding to soup

*Instead of ground beef, substitute turkey or chicken and add 2 Tbsp pesto in place of oregano.

Griddled Pesto Mozzarella Sandwich

YIELDS: 4 SANDWICHES

8 slices	Ciabatta Bread, 3/8 inch thick
As needed	Olive Oil
8 slices	Fresh Mozzarella, 1/4 inch thick
1/4 cup	Basil Pesto

- Slice bread and lay out on cutting board
- Brush tops of slices lightly with olive oil and turn over
- Spread a thin coating of pesto on each slice of bread
- Place mozzarella on 4 slices and top with the other slice of bread
- Heat a griddle over medium heat, place sandwich oil side down
- Grill until golden brown, about 2-3 minutes each side
- Cut and serve

FOR A FUN TWIST:

Substitute Basil Pesto for a Sundried Tomato Pesto, Lemon Artichoke Pesto or Black Olive Tapenade.

STRAWBERRY GAZPACHO SOUP

YIELDS: 1 1/2 QUARTS

MAKE THIS SOUP IN THE PEAK OF BERRY SEASON.

I FIND THAT ADDING MIXED BERRIES ADDS A CERTAIN DEPTH IN FLAVOR. However, you may prefer just strawberries. Both taste great, but remember to add the additional cup of strawberries to account for the mixed berry amount. Frozen berries are okay to substitute, but LOCAL BERRIES FROM THE FARMER'S MARKET WOULD BE BEST. Pair with a pitcher of margaritas!

2 1/2 cups	Strawberries
1 cup	Mixed Berries — Blueberries, Raspberries or Blackberries, strain for seeds
1/2 cup	Red Pepper, diced
1 cup	Cucumber, diced
1/4 cup	Onion, diced
1 Tbsp	Jalapeño, diced
1/2 tsp	Garlic, minced
1 Tbsp	Cilantro, rough chopped
2 Tbsp	Sherry Vinegar
1/2 cup	Water
1 Tbsp	Lime Juice - fresh
2 Tbsp	Orange Juice
1/2 tsp	Salt
2 Tbsp	Agave Nectar *(if needed)*
1/2 cup	Water *(if needed)*

GARNISH:

1 cup	Cucumber, minced
1/2 cup	Red Pepper, minced
1 Tbsp	Cilantro, finely chopped
1 cup	Strawberries, small diced

- Place all ingredients except garnish in blender and blend until smooth
- Adjust amount of water to reach the desired consistency
- Taste and add additional agave nectar depending on sweetness of the berries
- Fold in garnish
- Chill for at least 1 hour

Tequila Lime Chicken Salad

SERVES: 3 TO 4 PEOPLE

3 cups	Arugula
2	Tequila Grilled Chicken Breasts *(recipe below)*
1 cup	Grilled Red Bell Pepper*, julienne
1/4 cup	Tequila Lime Dressing *(page 135)*
1/4 cup	Toasted Pepitas *(Pumpkin Seeds)*

- Grill marinated chicken, then let it rest for 10 minutes and bias slice
- In a bowl, toss the arugula, grilled peppers and dressing
- Add chicken and lightly toss
- Top with toasted pepitas
- **Optional:** Add fresh orange or sprinkle top with queso blanco or jack cheese

*For a pop of color, use a trio of red, yellow and orange peppers.

Tequila Grilled Chicken

- Marinate chicken breasts for at least 30 minutes in the tequila lime dressing, then grill 8–10 minutes, until the internal temperature reaches 165°F

Jalapeño Fudge Brownies

YIELDS: 1 PAN

1 box	Brownie Mix (or favorite recipe)
1 Tbsp	Cinnamon - ground
1/4 cup	Jalapeño Jelly
8 oz	Cream Cheese, softened

- Mix cinnamon into your favorite brownie mix or recipe, pour into greased baking pan
- Blend jalapeño jelly with the softened cream cheese and dollop on the top of brownie mix
- With a butter knife, swirl the cream cheese mixture through the brownie mixture
- Follow baking instructions on the box or recipe and cool before serving

Beef + Bean Chili

CHILIES

There is nothing better on a chilly day THAN A BOWL OF CHILI simmering on the stove.

IT IS PERFECT FOR WATCHING FOOTBALL OR COMING HOME AFTER A DAY ON THE SLOPES.

The recipes that follow are medium to mild in heat.
Kick up the spice to the level that fits your personal taste buds.
There are lots of chilies on the market to experiment with or just increase the spices already listed.
Add another dimension to your chili and substitute beer for all or a portion of the stock listed in the recipe.
Be sure to give those flavors some time to simmer slowly on the stove so they can meld together.
I like to serve my chili with chopped onions, sour cream and cheese on the side.

Chili Bowl Ideas

QUINOA ON THE BOTTOM — top with chili, salsa and cheese

FRITO PIE — chili, Fritos, cheese, a dollop of sour cream and sprinkled with green onions

CHILI MAC — your favorite mac and cheese topped with chili, shaved jalapeños, a little cheese and choice of toppings

AMERICAN CHOP SUEY — chili tossed with cooked pasta and shredded cheese topped with sour cream, green onions, tomatoes and jalapeños

BEEF & BEAN CHILI

YIELDS: 2 1/2 QUARTS

1/4 cup	Canola Oil
2 lb	Ground Beef
1 Tbsp	Chili Powder
2 tsp	Cumin - ground
1 tsp	Paprika
1/4 tsp	Cinnamon - ground
1 tsp	Chipotle Powder
1/2 tsp	Black Pepper
1/2 tsp	Salt
1 1/2 tsp	Cocoa Powder
1 cup	Onions, diced
2 tsp	Garlic, minced
2 Tbsp	Flour
1 can (6 oz)	Tomato Paste
1/2 cup	Poblano Peppers, diced
1 can (14 oz)	Fire Roasted Tomatoes
1 can (15 oz)	Pinto Beans, drained and rinsed
2 cans (15 oz)	Kidney Beans, drained and rinsed
2 cups	Beef Stock *(page 130)* or Beer

- Heat a soup pot over medium-high heat and add canola oil
- Add ground beef and brown – do not overmix, beef needs to stay chunky
- When meat is 3/4 cooked, add the spices, finish cooking the meat and blooming the spices
- Add onions and garlic, cook until onions begin to sweat and become slightly translucent
- Add the poblano peppers
- Sprinkle flour and blend thoroughly into the mixture
- Add the tomato paste and cook mixture for 4 minutes
- Slowly add the beef stock and blend together, then add the tomatoes and beans
- Bring to a boil, reduce heat and simmer 15–20 minutes
- Season to taste with salt and pepper

WARM CORNBREAD & HONEY BUTTER, *(page 27)* **perfectly pair with a BOWL OF CHILI**

QUICK & EASY PULLED CHICKEN CHILI

YIELDS: 2 1/2 QUARTS

1/4 cup	Canola Oil
1 cup	Onions, diced
1 cup	Bell Peppers* *(red, yellow and orange)*, diced
1 tsp	Cumin - ground
1 tsp	Chili Powder
2 cups	Chunky Salsa Verde *(Chunky Green Chili Salsa)*
1 quart	Pulled Chicken *(leftover Rotisserie Chicken)*
1 cup	Water
1/4 cup	Cilantro
2 cans (15 oz)	Beans — Pinto, Kidney, Black or White, drained and rinsed

- Heat a soup pot over medium-high heat
- Add canola oil, sauté onions until they begin to sweat
- Add spices, cook for 2 minutes to bloom
- Add bell peppers, sauté until they begin to sweat
- Add chicken, salsa verde, water and beans
- Bring to a boil, reduce heat and simmer for 8–10 minutes
- Add cilantro, then season to taste with salt and pepper
- Simmer an additional 2 minutes

*For added heat, use poblano peppers as one of the three peppers or add 1 Tbsp jalapeños to the pepper mixture.

TURKEY & WHITE BEAN CHILI

YIELDS: 2 QUARTS

1/4 cup	Canola Oil
1 lb	Ground Turkey
1 cup	Onion, diced
2 tsp	Garlic, minced
4 tsp	Chili Powder
2 tsp	Cumin - ground
1 tsp	Paprika
1 tsp	Salt
1/2 tsp	Black Pepper
1/2 cup	Poblano Pepper, diced
1/4 cup	Red Bell peppers, diced
1/4 cup	Yellow Bell Peppers, diced
1/4 cup	Orange Bell Peppers, diced
1/2 cup	Corn
3 Tbsp	Flour
2 cans (15 oz)	White Beans, drained and rinsed
1 can (10 oz)	Diced Tomatoes with Green Chilies
3 cups	Chicken Stock *(page 130)*

- Heat a soup pot over medium-high heat with canola oil
- Add turkey, brown lightly, breaking it into pea-size pieces
- Once 3/4 cooked, add spices and cook 2 minutes to bloom
- Add onions and garlic, cook until they begin to sweat
- Add peppers and corn, cook until they begin to sweat
- Sprinkle flour and blend thoroughly into mixture, cook for 4 minutes
- Slowly add the chicken stock, blend well
- Add the tomatoes and beans
- Bring to a boil, reduce heat and simmer for 15 minutes
- Season to taste with salt and pepper
- **Optional:** Add cilantro; Add 2 Tbsp finely diced jalapeño or 1 habanero pepper when adding the garlic

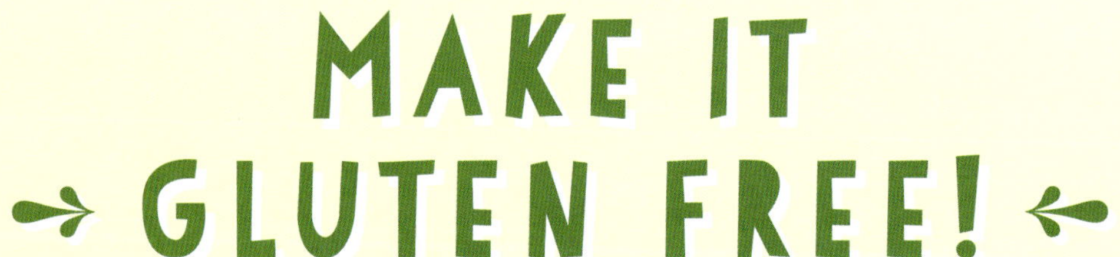

SUBSTITUTE FINELY GROUND CORNMEAL OR GLUTEN-FREE MASA HARINA FOR THE FLOUR.

Adobo Black Bean & Barley Chili

YIELDS: 2 1/2 QUARTS

1/4 cup	Canola Oil
1 cup	Onions, diced
1 tsp	Cumin - ground
2 tsp	Chili Powder
1 1/2 Tbsp	Chipotle in Adobo, pureed
1 tsp	Salt
1/4 cup	Celery, diced
1/2 cup	Carrots, diced
1/2 cup	Poblano Peppers, diced
1 1/2 cups	Bell Peppers *(red, yellow or orange)*, diced
1 1/2 cups	Zucchini and Yellow Squash, diced
1 cup	Corn
2 cans (15 oz)	Black Beans, drained and rinsed
1 can (14 oz)	Fire Roasted Tomatoes
3 Tbsp	Tomato Paste
1 cup	Barley *(pearl rapid cook)*
1 1/2 quarts	Vegetable Stock *(page 131)*
1 Tbsp	Honey *(substitute Agave Nectar)*
3 Tbsp	Cilantro
1	Lime, zest and juice

- Heat a soup pot over medium-high heat
- Add canola oil and onions, sauté until onions sweat
- Add spices, cook 2 minutes to bloom
- Add celery, carrots, peppers, squash and corn, sauté until vegetables begin to sweat
- Add tomato pasta and cook for 2 minutes
- Add tomatoes, beans and barley
- Add vegetable stock and honey
- Bring to a boil, reduce heat, and cook until barley is tender, about 12–15 minutes
- Add cilantro and lime
- Season to taste* with salt and pepper

*If chili is a little bitter due to vegetables, add 1 to 2 Tbsp honey.

STOCKS and BROTHS

Sipping Bone Broth is a trending healthy regimen.

EVEN THOUGH IT HAS BEEN AROUND FOREVER, advocates say that sipping bone broth daily can help fight off colds and flu, reduce joint pain and inflammation, aid in digestion, and strengthen skin, hair and nails. Bone broth contains gelatin, protein, and high amounts of antioxidants, vitamins and minerals. For an added healthful benefit, add fresh ginger or turmeric.

• • • • • Don't have time? • • • • •

Try using a slow cooker and let the bones simmer overnight.

A word about PURCHASING STOCK

As much as I would like to say I make all my stock, the reality is, unless I am making chicken soup, pho or have a turkey carcass from Thanksgiving, I rarely find the time, even though I know it does make a difference.

Not all stocks or bases are created equal, so be a label reader and try different varieties to find your favorite.

PURCHASE THE LOWER SODIUM VARIETIES.

You can always add salt, but I doubt you will find it necessary.

I usually purchase organic stocks, but that's my personal preference.

When stocks go on sale, I load up my pantry so they're on hand whenever I feel like making a quick soup.

I recommend making your own beef broth at least once.

It is time-consuming, but you'll find that sipping homemade beef broth with ginger is a truly delicious treat!

HOMEMADE STOCK TIPS

Keep a bag or two in your freezer to save vegetable trimmings or wilting vegetables to use for making stocks.

YOU'LL BE AMAZED HOW QUICKLY THE BAG WILL FILL UP!

The Basic Mirepoix consists of onions, carrots, celery, leeks, parsley and thyme stems, but you can also add mushrooms and tomatoes. Mirepoix vegetables are used for chicken and beef stocks.

Beef Stock

YIELDS: 2 QUARTS

2 to 2 1/2 lb Beef or Veal Bones *(shanks, ribs and shins)*
1 Onion, large diced
1-2 Carrots, large diced
1 rib Celery, large diced
2-3 Garlic Cloves
1 cup Tomato, large diced or ends and pieces
1 tsp Black Peppercorns
2 Bay Leaves
1 sprig Thyme - fresh

- Preheat oven to 400°F
- Place bones in a roasting pan, roast for 45 minutes, turning bones halfway through
- Add vegetables and herbs, return to the oven and continue roasting for at least 30 minutes, until the bones and vegetables turn brown
- Do not use chard or you will have a bitter stock
- Remove from oven, place in a stockpot and add 4 quarts of water
- Bring to a boil, reduce heat, and simmer for approximately 3 hours, until reduced by half
- Strain *(best through cheese cloth)*, cool and refrigerate

FOR GINGER BEEF BROTH:

- Omit thyme, bay leaves and tomatoes
- Add 1/4 lb fresh ginger, bias cut, 2-3 star anise, 1/4 bunch cilantro or 1/2 tsp coriander seeds
- Follow the same method
- **Optional:** Add an orange cut in quarters when you are adding water to the stockpot - do not roast

Chicken Stock

YIELDS: 2 1/2 QUARTS

5 lb Chicken *(legs, wings, necks, backs or bones)*
1 1/2 quarts Vegetables *(1 1/2 to 2 Carrots, 2 ribs Celery, 2 Medium Onions, 1/4 bunch Parsley Stems)*
2 Bay Leaves
1 sprig Thyme
1 tsp Black Peppercorns

- Rinse the chicken pieces
- Cut vegetables into large pieces
- Place chicken in soup pot, cover with water 1 inch above the bones, approximately 4 quarts
- Bring to a boil over medium heat and skim off the scum/impurities that form on top
- Add the vegetables, herbs and peppercorns, reduce heat and simmer
- Let cook for approximately 2-3 hours, remove any scum that forms on top
- Stock should reduce between 1/3 & 1/2
- Taste and continue simmering if flavor is watery
- Strain *(best through cheese cloth)* for less cloudy stock
- Refrigerator overnight so the fat solidifies on top and can be easily removed

Double Chicken Stock

YIELDS: 2 QUARTS

1 Whole Roasting Chicken
2 quarts Chicken Stock *(boxed or homemade)*
1 quart Water
1 quart Vegetables *(Onions, Carrots, Celery and Parsley Stems)*
1 sprig Thyme - fresh
2 Bay Leaves
1/2 tsp Black Peppercorns

- Rinse the chicken
- Cut vegetables into large pieces
- Place chicken in soup pot and cover with chicken stock and water
- Bring to a boil over medium heat, skim off the scum that forms on top
- Add vegetables, herbs and peppercorns, reduce heat and slowly simmer for approximately 2 hours, until reduced by 1/3
- Adjust seasoning to taste
- Strain *(best through cheese cloth)* for less cloudy stock
- Refrigerator overnight so the fat solidifies and can be easily removed

Turkey Stock *(page 44)*

Southwest Turkey Stock *(page 45)*

Mushroom Stock

YIELDS: 2 QUARTS

1/4 cup	Canola Oil
1 quart	Button Mushrooms
1 quart	Cremini or Portobello Mushrooms
1 pint	Shiitake Mushrooms
1	Onion
1	Carrot
1	Celery Rib, trimmed
2	Garlic Cloves, smashed
1 sprig	Thyme - fresh
1 sprig	Sage - fresh
1/4 bunch	Parsley Stems
1/2 cup	Red Wine
3 quarts	Water

- Preheat oven to 375°F
- Coat mushrooms and vegetables in canola oil, roast for 30 minutes
- Add herbs and red wine, roast 15-20 minutes, remove from oven
- Place all ingredients in a stockpot, rinse roasting pan and add to pot to get all the flavor
- Bring to a boil, reduce heat, simmer 30-45 minutes, until reduced by approximately 1/3
- Let sit for about 15 minutes, strain, cool and refrigerate

Fish Stock

YIELDS: 2 QUARTS

Ask your local fishmonger for some bones. Stick to bones from whitefish for a clean, light flavor.

3 lb	Fish Bones *(white fish only)*
2 cups	White Wine, dry not sweet
1	Leek *(white part only)*, large bias cut
1-2	Celery Ribs, large pieces
2	Bay Leaves
1/2 bunch	Parsley Stems
1 sprig	Thyme - fresh
1 tsp	Salt
1/4 tsp	Peppercorns
2 slices	Lemon
2 1/2 quarts	Water

- Place everything in a stockpot
- Bring to a boil, reduce heat, slowly simmer for 25-30 minutes, until reduced by approximately 1/4
- Strain (best through cheese cloth), let cool and refrigerate
- **Optional:** Add fennel depending on the soup you are making

(To keep the fish stock clear, stay away from vegetables like carrots, tomatoes and red onions.)

Vegetable Stock

YIELDS: 2 QUARTS

3 quarts	Vegetables *(Mushrooms, Onions/Leeks, Carrots, Celery, Tomato)*
1 quart	Optional Vegetables *(pick 2: Cabbage, Turnips, Squash, Fennel, Broccoli Stems, Asparagus Stems)*
2-3 cloves	Garlic, smashed
1/4 bunch	Parsley Stems
2	Bay Leaves
1 sprig	Thyme - fresh
1/2 tsp	Black Peppercorns

- Place vegetables in a soup pot
- Cover with 4 quarts water
- Bring to a boil, reduce heat, simmer for 45 minutes to 1 hour
- Water should reduce by half
- Remove from heat and let sit for 15 to 20 minutes, strain, cool and refrigerate

Roasted Vegetable Stock

YIELDS: 2 QUARTS

- Preheat oven to 375°F
- Toss vegetables in a little olive oil to barely coat
- Place in a roasting pan and roast about 30-45 minutes, until light brown*, stirring frequently throughout roasting time
- Remove vegetables from oven and place in a stockpot
- Using some of the water, rinse roasting pan and scrape all the flavor into stockpot
- Add herbs, 3 quarts of water and 1 cup of white wine *(optional)*
- Bring to a boil, reduce heat, and simmer 30-45 minutes, reducing the liquid by about 1/3
- Strain, let cool and refrigerate

*Do not let vegetables burn or you will have a very bitter stock!

Croutons
Salad Dressings

ADDITIONS

SALAD DRESSINGS

A tasty dressing can make a salad!

If you have a small blender or an immersion blender, making dressing is a snap and makes a big difference in even the simplest of salad. I try keeping extra virgin olive oil, canola oil, a good balsamic vinegar, rice wine vinegar, Dijon mustard, plain yogurt, fresh herbs, garlic, and citrus in my pantry.

There are some great dressings in the marketplace that use all natural gums and starches. This can help reduce calories and properly coat the greens. I keep a bottle or two of dressing on hand, and by simply adding an ingredient or two you can create a whole new flavor experience. When purchasing premade dressings, look for a simple vinaigrette with champagne, white balsamic or red wine vinegar without a lot of garlic or herbs.
Below are some quick and tasty dressings that can start with a bottled vinaigrette.
Just whisk the juice and spices together into the store-bought vinaigrette.

BELOW IS A BASIC VINAIGRETTE RECIPE IF YOU WANT TO MAKE IT FROM SCRATCH:

* If you find the basic dressing a little thin, add about 1 Tbsp of Dijon mustard
* *Substitute the juice for the canola oil in the recipes below — it could save a few calories.

BASIC VINAIGRETTE

YIELDS: 1 CUP

WHISK TOGETHER:

1/4 cup	Vinegar — Champagne, White Wine, Red Wine or White Balsamic
1/4 cup	Canola Oil*
1/2 cup	Extra Virgin Olive Oil
1/4 tsp	Salt
1/8 tsp	Black Pepper

For quick & easy: Place everything in a blender or use an immersion blender. Blend with 1 cup of Vinaigrette Dressing.

Chipotle Vinaigrette

- 1/4 cup Lime Juice*
- 1/4 tsp Chipotle in Adobo
- 1 Tbsp Cilantro

Pomegranate Vinaigrette

- 1/4 cup Pomegranate Juice or substitute Cranberry Juice*
- 1 Tbsp Honey
- 1/2 tsp Orange Zest
- 1 Tbsp Orange Juice

Harissa Vinaigrette

- 2 Tbsp Lemon Juice*
- 2 Tbsp Orange Juice*
- 2 tsp Harissa
- 1/2 tsp Orange Zest

Lemon Basil Vinnaigrette

- 1/4 cup Lemon Juice*
- 2 tsp Dijon Mustard
- 1 tsp Roasted Garlic
- 1-2 leaves Basil - fresh, chopped

Pesto Vinaigrette

- 1 1/2 Tbsp Basil Pesto
- 1 Tbsp Lemon Juice *(optional)*

Honey Mustard Vinaigrette

- 2 Tbsp Honey
- 2 Tbsp Dijon Mustard

[illegible] Vinaigrette

- 1/4 cup [illegible]
- 2 Tbsp Smoky Barbecue Sauce

Tomato Vinaigrette

- 1/4 cup V8 Juice
- Zest and juice from half a Lime
- 1/4 tsp Worcestershire Sauce
- 1 tsp Minced Jalapeño *(optional)*

Tangy Orange Vinaigrette

- 1 Tbsp Orange Marmalade
- 1/2 tsp Orange Zest
- 1 tsp Dijon Mustard *(optional)*

Caesar Dressing

YIELDS: 1 CUP

4	Anchovy Filets
1 tsp	Garlic, finely minced
1/8 tsp	Kosher Salt
1/8 tsp	Black Pepper
3 Tbsp	Lemon Juice - fresh
1 tsp	Dijon Mustard
2	Egg Yolks
1 tsp	Worcestershire Sauce
1/3 cup	Olive Oil
1/4 cup	Canola Oil
1 Tbsp	Water *(optional)*
3 Tbsp	Parmesan Cheese, finely grated

- Smash the anchovies and garlic together with salt and pepper to form a paste
- Add the lemon, mustard, Worcestershire and egg yolks and whisk together
- Slowly whisk in the oil, then add the cheese
- Add salt and pepper to taste
- **Make it easy:** Portion everything in a blender and blend.

Balsamic Vinaigrette

YIELDS: 1 CUP

1/2 tsp	Garlic, minced
1 Tbsp	Dijon Mustard
1/4 cup	Balsamic Vinegar
3/4 cup	Olive Oil
1/4 tsp	Salt
1/4 tsp	Black Pepper

- In a bowl, whisk garlic, mustard, balsamic vinegar, salt and pepper
- Slowly whisk in the oil until blended

SUBSTITUTIONS:

- Sherry vinegar for balsamic
- Replace 1/4 cup olive oil with cherry, orange or pomegranate juice
- **Make it easy:** Portion everything in a blender and blend.

1000 Island Dressing

YIELDS: 1 1/4 CUPS

BLEND TOGETHER:

2/3 cup	Mayonnaise*
1/4 cup	Ketchup
1/4 cup	Pickled Relish
11/2 tsp	Worcestershire Sauce
1/4 tsp	Black Pepper
To taste	Salt

*Depending on mayonnaise, you may need a touch of lemon juice.

Avocado Ranch

YIELDS: 1 1/2 CUPS

BLEND TOGETHER:

1 cup	Ranch Dressing
1/2 cup	Avocado, smashed
1 Tbsp	Cilantro
1 Tbsp	Lime Juice - fresh

OPTIONAL:

2 Tbsp	Salsa
1 1/2 tsp	Fresh Jalapeños, minced
1/2 tsp	Chipotle in Adobo, pureed
1 Tbsp	Roasted Poblano Pepper

Warm Bacon Dressing

YIELDS: 1/2 CUP (ABOUT 4 SERVINGS)

1/2 cup	Thick Cut Bacon, julienne
1/4 cup	Onions, diced
1/2 tsp	Garlic, minced
2 tsp	Sugar
1/4 tsp	Black Pepper
1/2 to 1 tsp	Dijon Mustard
1/4 cup	Red Wine Vinegar

- Cook bacon in a sauté pan over medium heat, remove bacon and set aside
- Add onions to bacon drippings *(should have 3-4 Tbsp, add Olive Oil if necessary)* and sauté
- Add garlic, let it bloom, then add sugar, mustard and black pepper
- Add the red wine vinegar, let simmer about 1 1/2 minutes and pour over a bowl of spinach or greens

Tequila Lime Dressing

YIELDS: 1 CUP

1/4 cup	Lime Juice
1 tsp	Lime Zest
2 Tbsp	Tequila
1 Tbsp	Red Onion or Shallot
3/4 cup	Olive Oil *(substitute a portion of canola oil)*
1/4 tsp	Kosher Salt
1/4 tsp	Chipotle Powder
1 Tbsp	Cilantro
2 tsp	Agave Nectar

- Blend all ingredients except for oil and cilantro in a bowl
- Slowly add the olive oil until blended, then fold in the cilantro
- **Make it easy:** Portion everything in a blender and blend.

CROUTONS

CROUTONS ADD A GREAT CRUNCH AND FLAVOR TO ANY SALAD OR SOUP!

I LIKE TO EXPERIMENT WITH DIFFERENT TYPES OF BREADS FOR ADDED FLAVOR AND TEXTURE LIKE PUMPERNICKEL BREAD WITH THE LEMON DILL CROUTON RECIPE. Day-old bread is best for croutons. If you can't use the bread right away, cube it, place in a Ziploc® bag and store in the freezer. I usually use the oven method to make croutons, since I always burn them on the stove. The oven method is quick, easy and I can set a timer and walk away.

Crouton Oven Method

YIELDS: 1 QUART

4 cups	Bread, 1/2-inch cubes
3–4 Tbsp	Garlic Oil *(page 137)*
1 tsp	Salt
1/4 tsp	Black Pepper

- Preheat oven to 375°F
- Whisk oil, salt and pepper together, then toss with cubed bread
- Spread a single layer on a baking sheet and bake for 10 minutes
- Stir for even baking, then continue to bake for 8–12 minutes, until golden brown

Crouton Stovetop Method

YIELDS: 1 QUART

4 cups	Bread, 1/2-inch cubes
2 Tbsp	Butter
2 Tbsp	Olive Oil or Garlic Oil *(page 137)*
1/2 tsp	Salt

- Over medium-high heat, add butter and canola oil to a large sauté pan
- Add bread cubes, sprinkle with salt and pepper, then sauté until crisp and golden brown
- Remove croutons from the sauté pan and place on paper towels to absorb any excess oil

Lemon Dill Croutons

ADD:

1/2 tsp	Lemon Zest
1/2 tsp	Dill or Thyme - fresh

Lemon Pepper Croutons

ADD:

1/2 tsp	Lemon Zest
1/2 tsp	Black Pepper

Dijon Croutons

ADD:

1 tsp	Dijon Mustard
1 tsp	Parsley, chopped

Spicy Sriracha Croutons

ADD:

1 tsp	Sriracha Sauce

Parmesan Croutons

TOSS WARM CROUTONS IN:

2 Tbsp	Grated Parmesan

Cilantro Lime Croutons

ADD:

1/2 tsp	Lime Zest
1/2 tsp	Lime Juice - fresh
1 tsp	Cilantro, chopped

GARLIC OIL

YIELDS: 1 CUP

1 cup	Olive Oil
1 Tbsp	Garlic Cloves, shaved
1/4 tsp	Lemon Zest *(optional)*

- Place oil and shaved garlic in a pan and slowly heat pan over medium heat, until garlic becomes soft and tender
- Remove from heat and add lemon zest

Grilled Crostini Bread

- Brush slices of crusty bread with garlic oil, sprinkle with salt and pepper
- Griddle both sides until they are golden brown
- **Optional:** Place on sheet pan, bake in a 375° for 12-15 minutes or until golden brown

ICE CREAM TOPPINGS

ICE CREAM IS ALWAYS A POPULAR, EASY DESSERT.
Here are a few tasty toppings for your favorite ice cream. Finish with toasted nuts or nutty granola *(page 97)*. Try these toppings with plain or vanilla Greek yogurt.

Chocolate Sauce

YIELDS: 1 QUART

2 cups	Heavy Cream
1 cup	Chocolate Chips
1/2 cup	Cocoa
1/2 to 3/4 cup	Water
1/2 cup	Sugar
1/4 cup	Orange Juice*
1 tsp	Pure Vanilla Extract or 1/4 Vanilla Bean

- Mix cocoa and sugar in a saucepan with water, then add heavy cream and orange juice
- Over medium heat, bring mixture to a light simmer and cook for 2 minutes *(do not boil)*
- Fold in the chocolate chips and vanilla until blended
- **Optional:** Add cinnamon, cayenne or chipotle pepper

*Substitute coffee/espresso for orange juice.

Baked Bananas

SERVES: 6 TO 8 PEOPLE

3 to 4	Bananas, split lengthwise
1	Orange, juice
1 Tbsp	Rum *(optional)*
1/2 tsp	Cinnamon
1/4 tsp	Nutmeg
1/4 tsp	Crystallized Ginger, minced
1 Tbsp	Brown Sugar
1 tsp	Butter, melted
4 Tbsp	Nutty Granola

- Preheat oven to 400°F
- Spray baking dish, arrange bananas in bottom
- Mix orange, rum, butter, sugar and spices
- Spoon mixture over top of bananas
- Sprinkle with Nutty Granola
- Bake for 12-15 minutes

Blueberry Lemon Curd

YIELDS: 1 CUP

3	Egg Yolks
1/2 cup	Sugar
1/3 cup	Lemon Juice
2 tsp	Lemon Zest
3 Tbsp	Butter, unsalted
1 Tbsp	Cornstarch, blended with 1/4 cup water
1 cup	Fresh Blueberries

- In a saucepan, whisk egg yolks, sugar, lemon zest and juice
- Cook over medium heat, whisking continually until mixture bubbles in the center
- Add cornstarch and cook 3-4 minutes
- Remove from heat and fold in butter and blueberries
- Cover and cool or spoon warm over ice cream

Quick & Easy Salted Caramel Sauce

YIELDS: 1 CUP

1/2 cup	Brown Sugar
1/2 cup	Granulated Sugar
1/2 cup	Heavy Cream
1 stick	Butter, unsalted
1/2 tsp	Kosher Salt
1/2 tsp	Pure Vanilla Extract or 1/4 Vanilla Bean

- Place everything in a saucepan
- Over medium-high heat, bring to a boil
- Reduce heat and simmer for 8-10 minutes
- Remove vanilla bean and serve

Pineapple Coconut

YIELDS: 2 CUPS

1 cup	Crushed Pineapple *(in juice not syrup)*
1 can	Mandarin Oranges
1 cup	Toasted Coconut
1	Lime, zest and juice

- Drain the mandarin oranges, place in a bowl
- Add crushed pineapple with juice, toasted coconut and lime
- Toss and let sit for 30 minutes
- **Optional:** Add 1 tsp Crystallized Ginger or 1/2 tsp Cinnamon

Peanut Butter Crunch

YIELDS: 2 1/4 CUPS

1 cup	Heavy Cream
1/2 cup	Peanut Butter Powder
1/4 cup	Water
3 Tbsp	Honey
1 Tbsp	Cornstarch, blended with 1/4 cup water
1/4 tsp	Kosher Salt
1 cup	Dry Roasted Peanuts, finely chopped

- In a saucepan, heat cream, peanut butter powder and water, bring to a boil, simmer for 2-3 minutes
- Fold in honey, salt and cornstarch, cook 2 minutes, then fold in dry roasted peanuts

Smashed Strawberry Lime Basil

YIELDS: 2 CUPS

2 cups	Fresh Strawberries
1	Lime, zest and juice
2 Tbsp	Sugar, granulated
1 Tbsp	Basil* - fresh, chopped

- Toss everything in a bowl and lightly smash the strawberries
- Let sit for at least 1 hour to macerate
- **Optional:** Add a kick with a shot of your favorite tequila or rum to the marinade

*Substitute mint or thyme for basil.

NUTS

Simple Toasted Nuts

TOASTING NUTS INTENSIFIES THE FLAVORS. By activating the oils, you get a crispier texture, richer color and it helps to reduce the bitter notes found it some nuts, like walnuts. I prefer the oven method of toasting since I have a tendency to burn them on the stovetop. Fresh from the oven is best, but I usually make extra and keep in a tightly sealed container. The toasted nuts make a great snack as well as salad topper.

Stovetop Toasting

- In a dry sauté pan over medium-high heat, sauté nuts for 3–5 minutes
- Stir frequently for even toasting

Oven Toasting

- Preheat oven to 350°F
- Spread a single layer of nuts on a baking sheet or pan, toast for 5 minutes, remove from oven and stir for even toasting, return to oven and toast for an additional 5–7 minutes, until golden brown
- Remove from the oven and let cool

ADD SOME SPICE TO THE TOASTING PROCESS:

- Soak the nuts via the oven candied nut recipe below and toss with salt and your favorite spice
- Roast in the oven for 15–18 minutes

Candied Nuts

CANDIED NUTS ADD THAT SPECIAL TOUCH TO A SALAD, CHEESE OR SNACKING TRAY. An array of recipes to get you started are on the next page. Start with the Basic Recipe as a base and be creative with your own spice combination. In the stovetop method, you can substitute liquor or hot sauce for the water.

Stovetop

- In a dry pan, begin to toast nuts, stir so they don't burn
- When nuts begin to change color and get a nice nutty smell, add 1 Tbsp butter and cook for about 1 minute
- Add sugar and spice mixture from recipes below and 1–2 Tbsp water
- Continue cooking until the sauce thickens and is coating the nuts
- Remove from heat, spread out on a parchment- or foil-lined pan, separate pieces with a fork
- Cool and let sugar harden
- Store in a sealed container

Oven

- Preheat oven to 350°F
- In a bowl, cover the nuts with hot water and let sit for a minimum of 5 minutes
- Drain and lightly pat dry with paper towels
- In a bowl, toss sugar mixture *(page 141)* with nuts until nicely coated
- Spread out on a parchment- or foil-lined sheet pan
- Place in oven and roast for 18–22 minutes, stirring at least once during the roasting process, until nuts turn a nice golden brown
- Remove from heat and let cool, break apart and store in sealed container

 SPICED SUGAR RECIPES ARE BASED ON 1 CUP OF SOAKED NUTS 

Basic

- 1/4 cup — **Sugar**
- 1/8 tsp — **Cayenne**
- 1 tsp — **Salt**

Chipotle Lime

- 1/4 cup — **Sugar**
- 1/4 tsp — **Chipotle Powder**
- 1/2 tsp — **Lime Zest**
- 1 tsp — **Salt**

Spiced

- 1/4 cup — **Sugar**
- 1/2 tsp — **Cinnamon**
- 1/4 tsp — **Cumin**
- 1/8 tsp — **Cayenne**
- 1 tsp — **Salt**

Ginger Orange

- 1/4 cup — **Sugar**
- 1 tsp — **Ginger**
- 1/2 tsp — **Orange Zest**
- 1/4 tsp — **Cayenne**
- 1 tsp — **Salt**

Curry

- 1/4 cup — **Sugar**
- 3/4 tsp — **Curry Powder**
- 1/4 tsp — **Cayenne**
- 1 tsp — **Salt**

SOUPS FOR EVERY OCCASION

it all starts with a pot of soup!

Whether it's 80 degrees or 20, sunny or rainy, there's always a perfect bowl of soup to be the "STAR" of a meal.

Light, bright or chilled soups are perfect for hot days, while hearty soups take the chill out of days that are cold and gray. Soups can be great to offer that healthy halo, but when a bit of indulgence is needed, velvety cream soups are "just what the doctor ordered." And classics simply work all year round.

Once you make a soup selection, meal planning is easy. Pick a salad, sandwich and/or bread . . . then add a finishing touch such as fruit, ice cream or nuts.

The following pages provide thought-starters for matching a soup to common needs and situations.

Ideas for Different Occasions

QUICK HEALTHY LUNCHES FOR THE OFFICE

- Moroccan Chicken & Vegetable
- Aztec Chicken Soup
- Turkey & White Bean Chili
- Lentil, Tomato & Eggplant
- Spring Greens
- Adobo Black Bean & Barley Chili
- Simple Gazpacho

PARTY TIME

- Taco Soup
- Buffalo Chicken Soup
- Escarole Sausage & Tortellini
- New England Clam Chowder in bread boules
- Grilled Vegetable Barley
- Corn Chowder
- Loaded Sweet Potato
- Holiday Soup

SPECIAL OCCASIONS

- New Year's Black-Eyed Pea
- Matzo Ball
- Oysters Rockefeller
- Harira
- Seafood Bisque
- Holiday Soup
- Thanksgiving Turkey

DINNER AL FRESCO

- Asparagus Soup
- Gazpacho
- Creamy Lemon Chicken & Rice
- Roasted Poblano & Corn Bisque
- Seafood Bisque
- Ranch Steak Soup
- Curried Zucchini
- Roasted Tomato Basil Soup

CLASSIC ANYTIME FAVORITES

- Mom's Chicken Noodle
- Tomato
- Minestrone
- Beef Mushroom Barley
- Chicken Pot Pie
- Broccoli Cheese
- Split Pea & Ham
- Three Onion

Seasonal Favorites

SPRING & SUMMER

- Asparagus
- Carrot Fennel
- Creamy Lemon Chicken Rice
- Leek & Potato
- Spring Greens
- Aztec Chicken
- Coconut Fish Chowder
- Corn Chowder
- Ranch Steak
- Simple Gazpacho
- Roasted Tomato Basil
- Strawberry Gazpacho
- Grilled Vegetable Barley
- Curried Zucchini
- Chilled Avocado
- Roasted Poblano & Corn Bisque

FALL & WINTER

- Beef Mushroom Barley
- Beef & Bean Chili
- Adobo Black Bean
- Butternut Squash & Apple Bisque
- Cabbage Patch
- Chicken Pot Pie
- Classic Tomato
- Curried Pumpkin
- Escarole Sausage & Tortellini
- Loaded Sweet Potato
- Mushroom, Leek & Apple
- Senate Bean Soup
- Spinach, Bacon & Mushroom
- Red Beans & Rice
- Three Onion
- Split Pea & Ham
- Quick Pho

ALL SEASON SOUPS

- Broccoli Cheese
- Classic Minestrone
- Classic Tomato
- Beef & Bean Chili
- Cream of Cauliflower
- Garden Vegetable
- New England Clam Chowder
- Quick & Easy Pulled Chicken Chili
- Egg Drop
- Mom's Chicken Noodle
- Roasted Eggplant & Tomato Bisque

ALL SEASON SOUPS (cont.)

- Pulled Buffalo Chicken
- Quick Pho
- Adobo Black Bean & Barley Chili
- Turkey Posole
- Taco Soup
- Thai Coconut
- Italian Stracciatella
- Turkey & White Bean Chili
- Lentil, Tomato & Eggplant
- Black Bean & Chorizo Sausage
- Egg Drop

Perfect for Holiday Entertaining

NEW YEAR'S

- Black-Eyed Pea
- Oysters Rockefeller Bisque

SUPER BOWL

- Pulled Buffalo Chicken
- Taco Soup
- Chili

CHINESE NEW YEAR

- Quick Pho
- Pulled Chinese Chicken Vegetable
- Egg Drop
- Thai Coconut

VALENTINE'S DAY

- Seafood Bisque
- Three Onion
- Spinach, Bacon & Mushroom

MARDI GRAS

- Red Beans & Rice

EASTER

- Carrot Fennel
- Asparagus
- Leek & Potato
- Creamy Lemon Chicken & Rice

PASSOVER

- Matzo Ball
- Spring Greens

Perfect for Holiday Entertaining (cont.)

CINCO DE MAYO

Avocado Soup

- Taco Soup
- Turkey Posole

MEMORIAL DAY

- Roasted Poblano & Corn Bisque
- Roasted Tomato Basil Soup

4th OF JULY

- Simple Gazpacho
- Strawberry Gazpacho
- New England Clam Chowder

LABOR DAY

- Corn Chowder
- Simple Gazpacho

ELECTION DAY

- Senate Bean Soup

THANKSGIVING

- Butternut Squash & Apple Bisque
- Curried Pumpkin
- Mushroom, Leek & Apple Bisque

RAMADAN

- Harira

CHRISTMAS

- Holiday Soup
- Spinach, Bacon & Mushroom
- Butternut Squash & Apple Bisque

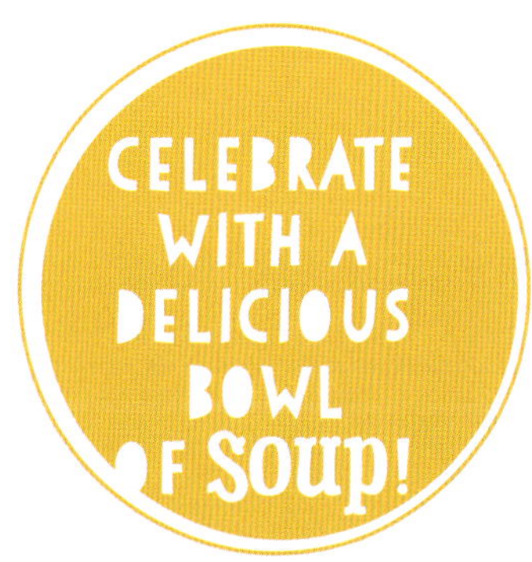

SOUP NUTRITIONAL GUIDE

THE FOLLOWING NUTRITIONAL INFORMATION IS ONLY A GUIDE*

WITH THE MASSIVE ARRAY OF MANUFACTURED INGREDIENTS TO CHOOSE FROM

CALORIES COULD VARY.

ALSO DOUBLE CHECK ANY PRE-PREPARED ITEMS THAT THEY ARE COMPLETELY GLUTEN FREE OR VEGAN.

NOTE: **I did not include the SODIUM LEVELS in this guide. These numbers vary to greatly depending on which ingredient you choose.**

To watch sodium levels choose the "low" or "no sodium added" in items like canned tomatoes, beans and manufactured stocks.

**This information was generated using the ReciPal nutritional program and based on a 1 cup serving unless specifed.*

SOUPS	SERV. SIZE	CAL.	FAT CAL.	TOTAL FAT	SAT. FAT	TRANS FAT	PRO-TEIN	SUGAR	FIBER	VG	V	GF	CW
Adobo Black Bean	1 cup	230	35	3.5g	0g	0g	13g	9g	8g	✓	✓	✓	
Adobo Black Bean w/ Corn Salsa	1 cup	240	35	3.5g	0g	0g	13g	10g	8g	✓	✓	✓	
Asparagus	1 cup	230	120	13g	7g	0g	6g	11g	3g		✓		
Aztec Chicken	1 cup	200	100	11g	1.5g	1g	9g	5g	2g			✓	✓
Beef Mushroom Barley	1 cup	180	45	5g	0.5g	0g	12g	4g	3g	✓	✓		✓
Black Bean & Chorizo Sausage	1 cup	210	90	10g	3g	0g	13g	3g	7g			✓	✓
Broccoli Cheese	1 cup	190	110	12g	4.5g	0g	7g	2g	2g		✓		✓
Butternut Squash & Apple Bisque	1 cup	180	110	13g	4g	0g	2g	10g	2g		✓	✓	✓
Cabbage Patch	1 cup	190	110	12g	3g	0g	8g	5g	2g			✓	✓
Carrot Fennel	1 cup	160	90	10g	3g	0g	2g	6g	3g		✓		✓
Chicken Pot Pie	1 cup	260	140	16g	5g	1g	9g	3g	2g				
Chicken Pot Pie w/ Crumbled Crust	1/8 recipe	450	240	27g	9g	2g	12g	5g	4g				
Chilled Avocado	1 cup	200	130	15g	2g	0g	7g	3g	8g		✓	✓	✓
Classic Minestrone	1 cup	210	110	12g	3g	0g	10g	3g	3g		✓		✓
Classic Tomato	1 cup	160	70	8g	3g	0g	2g	17g	3g	✓	✓	✓	✓
Coconut Fish Chowder	1 cup	330	230	26g	15g	0g	17g	3g	2g			✓	
Corn Chowder	1 cup	250	120	14g	7g	0g	7g	5g	2g		✓		
Corn Chowder w/ Bacon	1 cup	310	180	20g	9g	1g	9g	5g	2g				
Corn Chowder w/ Chicken & Bacon	1 cup	330	190	21g	8g	1.5g	11g	4g	5g				
Corn Chowder w/ Lobster	1 cup	260	130	14g	7g	0g	10g	5g	2g				
Corn Chowder w/ Poblano	1 cup	250	130	14g	7g	0g	7g	5g	3g		✓		
Corn Chowder w/ Shrimp	1 cup	270	130	14g	7g	0g	12g	5g	2g				
Corn Chowder w/ Smoked Salmon	1 cup	240	120	13g	6g	0g	9g	4g	2g				
Creamy Lemon Chicken & Rice	1 cup	330	180	20g	10g	0g	9g	8g	12g			✓	
Cream of Cauliflower	1 cup	300	150	16g	10g	0.5g	12g	17g	3g	✓	✓		
Curried Pumpkin	1 cup	270	220	24g	14g	0g	4g	6g	4g	✓	✓	✓	
Curried Zucchini	1 cup	300	230	25g	17g	0g	3g	13g	2g		✓		
Egg Drop	1 cup	210	110	12g	2.5g	0g	17g	1g	<1g				✓
Escarole Sausage & Tortellini	1 cup	200	80	9g	2.5g	0g	12g	3g	2g				✓
Garden Vegetable	1 cup	90	35	4g	0g	0g	3g	5g	2g	✓	✓	✓	✓
Grilled Vegetable Barley	1 cup	160	60	7g	0.5g	0g	4g	11g	5g	✓	✓		
Holiday Soup (Mini Meatball 3 each)	1 cup	150	90	10g	3g	0g	9g	2g	1g				✓
Harira	1 cup	300	110	12g	2g	0g	23g	5g	7g				
Italian Stracciatella	1 cup	180	100	11g	2.5g	0g	15g	<1g	2g			✓	✓
Leek & Potato	1 cup	260	140	15g	10g	0.5g	6g	3g	3g		✓		
Lentil, Tomato & Eggplant	1 cup	170	50	6g	0g	0g	9g	7g	9g	✓	✓	✓	✓
Loaded Sweet Potato	1 cup	290	180	20g	7g	1.5g	7g	8g	2g			✓	

SOUPS (cont.)	SERV. SIZE	CAL.	FAT CAL.	TOTAL FAT	SAT. FAT	TRANS FAT	PRO-TEIN	SUGAR	FIBER	VG	V	G	C
Matzo Ball w/ 2 matzo balls	1 cup	230	110	12g	2g	0g	13g	4g	<1g			✓	
Mom's Chicken Noodle	1 cup	160	60	6g	1g	0g	10g	4g	<1g				✓
Moroccan Chicken Vegetable	1 cup	190	80	9g	1g	0.5g	8g	3g	3g		🍃	✓	✓
Mushroom, Leek & Apple Bisque	1 cup	220	130	14g	6g	0g	5g	7g	2g		✓		✓
New England Clam Chowder	1 cup	290	200	22g	11g	1.5g	9g	2g	1g				
New Year's Black-Eyed Pea	1 cup	160	60	6g	0.5g	0g	12g	4g	5g		🍃	✓	✓
Oysters Rockefeller Bisque	1 cup	360	150	16g	8g	0g	21g	5g	2g				
Pulled Buffalo Chicken	1 cup	230	110	12g	2g	0g	16g	3g	2g				
Pulled Chinese Chicken Vegetable	1 cup	140	70	7g	1g	0g	11g	2g	2g				✓
Quick Pho	1/4 recipe	470	110	12g	3.5g	0g	39g	11g	4g	🍃	🍃		
Ranch Steak	1 cup	220	80	9g	1g	0g	15g	7g	3g				✓
Red Beans & Rice	1 cup	230	100	11g	3.5g	1g	10g	2g	3g			✓	
Roasted Eggplant & Tomato Bisque	1 cup	204	114	13g	6g	0g	4g	7g	5g		✓		✓
Roasted Poblano & Corn Bisque	1 cup	210	120	14g	5g	0g	5g	6g	2g		✓		✓
Roasted Tomato Basil	1 cup	90	25	3g	0g	0g	3g	11g	2g	🍃	✓	✓	✓
Seafood Bisque	1 cup	360	210	23g	13g	0.5g	22g	3g	<1g				
Senate Bean	1 cup	330	90	10g	3.5g	1g	21g	4g	14g			✓	
Simple Gazpacho	1 cup	90	45	5g	0.5g	0g	2g	7g	3g	✓	✓	✓	✓
Spinach, Bacon & Mushroom	1 cup	290	200	23g	9g	2g	11g	2g	4g				
Split Pea & Ham	1 cup	310	90	10g	1.5g	0g	25g	4g	15g		🍃	✓	
Spring Greens	1 cup	110	40	4.5g	0g	0g	3g	5g	4g	✓	✓	✓	✓
Strawberry Gazpacho	1 cup	120	0	0.5g	0g	0g	2g	20g	4g	✓	✓	✓	✓
Taco Soup	1 cup	280	120	13g	4.5g	0g	17g	5g	6g				
Thanksgiving Turkey	1 cup	140	50	6g	1g	0g	6g	5g	1g				✓
Thai Coconut	1 cup	210	140	16g	8g	0.5g	7g	2g	1g			✓	✓
Three Onion	1 cup	220	110	12g	6g	0g	8g	9g	2g		🍃		✓
Turkey Posole	1 cup	230	80	9g	1.5g	0g	15g	7g	3g			✓	

CHILI	SERV. SIZE	CAL.	FAT CAL.	TOTAL FAT	SAT. FAT	TRANS FAT	PRO-TEIN	SUGAR	FIBER	VG	V	G	C
Adobo Black Bean & Barley	1 cup	260	60	7g	0.5g	0g	10g	9g	11g	🍃	✓		
Beef & Bean	1 cup	390	140	16g	4.5g	0.5g	29g	5g	10g				
Turkey & White Bean	1 cup	330	110	13g	2g	0g	22g	4g	7g			✓	
Quick & Easy Pulled Chicken	1 cup	270	130	14g	2g	0g	20g	7g	3g				

NUTRITIONAL GUIDE KEY

 = soup ingredients can be adjusted to be **Vegetarian** or **Vegan**

VG = **Vegan** – all plant-based ingredients with nothing derived from an animal

V = **Vegetarian** – vegan with dairy and eggs added

G = **Gluten Free** – items do not contain gluten
— double check any pre-prepared items that they are completely gluten free

C = **Calorie Wise** – soups that are 225 calories or less for a 1 cup serving

A POT OF soup
SIMMERING ON THE STOVE
IS comfort AT
ITS best.

Visit Becky's website
to see what's COOKING!
CookingSoupToNuts.com

NOTES

NOTES

NOTES